D0228758

VOTES FOR WOMEN!

Praise for Jenni Murray's
A History of Britain in 21 Women

'Murray tells their remarkable stories with her own extraordinary wit, passion and piercing insight. She is the perfect guide.'

Helen Castor

'I can't think of any more seductive way of learning about the past than meeting its principals as if they were friends in a room. That's the gift that Jenni Murray gives us; a rare gift because these principals are women. If someone in every country were to write a book like this, scholars might finally admit there are two things – history and the past – and they are not the same.'

Gloria Steinem

'I was fascinated by this well-researched, informative and entertaining book. I knew the names of many of the women among its pages, but not their stories and it was wonderful to read about them via Jenni Murray's warm and well-written prose. Entertaining, enjoyable and scholarly.'

Elizabeth Chadwick, bestselling author of the *Eleanor of Aquitaine* trilogy

'Jenni Murray has invited us to her feast of extraordinary women … As incomparable host, Jenni lets her guests display themselves lavishly, telling their own noble or quirky stories while she delicately inserts anecdotes from her own distinguished life. This is no closed event. The book invites us all to come in. It's a feast you won't want to miss!'

Janet Todd, professor emerita, University of Aberdeen, and author of *Death and the Maidens*

'A fresh and very timely way of looking at British history, illuminated by Murray's own incomparable experience in the world of women's stories. Her twenty-one vignettes – of well-known and little-known alike – benefit from the blend of warmth and scepticism that has long marked her own contribution to national life.'

Sarah Gristwood

'*A History of Britain in 21 Women* is impossible to put down or ignore. The legendary Jenni Murray opens up the lives of great figures living and long dead. The veteran interviewer's voice is present throughout; probing, challenging but never drowning out her well-chosen subjects. The book is dedicated to the young but offers so much to women and men of all ages.'

Shami Chakrabarti

'Ideal to press into the hands of young women studying politics and history.'

Independent

'The value she gives those presently underrated qualities, patience and fortitude, will stand a lifetime's reference.'

Telegraph

Emmeline Pankhurst arrested in front of
Buckingham Palace, 1914.

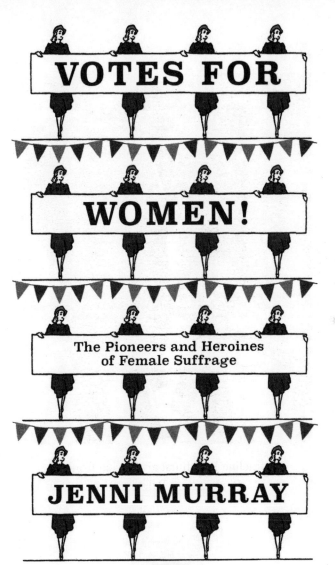

VOTES FOR

WOMEN!

The Pioneers and Heroines of Female Suffrage

JENNI MURRAY

ONEWORLD

A Oneworld Book

First published by Oneworld Publications, 2018

Chapters on Mary Wollstonecraft, Elizabeth Garrett Anderson,
Millicent Garrett Fawcett, Emmeline Pankhurst, Constance Markievicz
and Nancy Astor first published by Oneworld Publications in
A History of Britain in 21 Women, 2016

A CIP record for this title is available from the British Library

ISBN 978-1-78607-475-1
eISBN 978-1-78607-476-8

Printed and bound in Great Britain by Clays Ltd, St Ives plc

Oneworld Publications
10 Bloomsbury Street
London WC1B 3SR
England

Stay up to date with the latest books,
special offers, and exclusive content from
Oneworld with our newsletter

Sign up on our website
oneworld-publications.com

MIX
Paper from
responsible sources
FSC® C018072
www.fsc.org

I thank my Grandmother, Edna Jones, who taught me what I want the next generation of girls to know – your vote counts.

'My own sex, I hope, will excuse me, if I treat them like rational creatures, instead of flattering their fascinating graces, and viewing them as if they were in a state of perpetual childhood, unable to stand alone.'

Mary Wollstonecraft

'[The Government] will tear the stars from the sky before they break the spirit of women in this country.'

Christabel Pankhurst

'I incite this meeting to rebellion.'

Emmeline Pankhurst

'Other movements towards freedom have aimed at raising the status of a comparatively small group or class. But the women's movement aims at nothing less than raising the status of an entire sex – half the human race – to lift it up to the freedom and valour of womanhood.'

Millicent Garrett Fawcett

'I have all my life felt very strongly the injustice and stupidity of keeping women out of any kind of work, for which they happened to be indubitably fit, and of making any distinction between them and men, once they were admitted.'

Millicent Garrett Fawcett

Contents

I never knew you; never came within the
    sphere
Of that most radiant personality
I rarely thought of you, nor knew I held
    you dear
Nor realised for what you stood to me;
For what I breathed in with my native air
For womanhood enfranchised, educated,
    free.

'A Modern Girl to Mrs Pankhurst'

Introduction

2018 and it's one hundred years since women finally kicked down the doors of Britain's exclusively male Parliament, won the right to vote for their chosen MP and stand for election. In evolutionary terms it's a very short period of time, and it was to some degree only a partial triumph after a long, hard battle. It has to be described as a *partial* triumph because the 1918 Representation of the People Act, enacted on 6 February that year, permitted access to the ballot box to only the most privileged women.

While all men over the age of twenty-one gained the right to vote, women had to be at least thirty, and there were further hurdles. To be included, a woman had to be a member of the Local Government Register or the wife of a member or a property owner or a graduate voting in the constituency of her university. Universal suffrage, which granted equal rights to men and women over the age of twenty-one, would not be won for another ten years.

Despite the restrictions the electorate rose from 7.7 million to 21.4 million, and women, in the first election to follow the Act, held on 14 December 1918, thronged to the polls. Newly enfranchised, they now made up 43 per cent of the electorate. But why that thirty-year-old rule? Some believed it reflected the still widely held belief that women and children were similarly incompetent when it came to the consideration of the important issues of the day. More likely it was a reaction to the terrible reduction in the number of potential male voters, as so many men had perished in the Great War. As it was clear that, even with the age and property restrictions, the female turnout could have made for 50 per cent of votes cast, something had to be done to keep the numbers down. It would never have done for women to form the majority!

Nevertheless, the winning of the vote, despite the limitations, was a phenomenal event. And yes, I insist on the use of the words *won* or *winning*. We must never make the mistake of diminishing the achievement of the campaigners by assuming women were *given* or *granted* the vote. They fought for it! There had been years and years of an ever-more determined and angry drive to ensure that women should enjoy the basic human right to take a full part in the democratic process and choose by whom they were governed. As the American colonists put it in the years before the revolution against British rule, 'Taxation without representation is tyranny.'

It was in 1792 that British women were first given the opportunity to read a book that pointed them in the direction of equality with men. Mary Wollstonecraft's *A Vindication of the Rights of Woman* is the first genuinely feminist tome. She rails at women's lack of education, their difficulty in finding work and want of financial independence, and their reliance on marriage for their comforts and status. As for political engagement, she wrote, 'There must be more equality established in society, or morality will never gain ground, and this virtuous equality will not rest firmly even when founded on a rock, if one half of mankind be chained to its bottom by fate.'

It was Wollstonecraft's work that inspired the women who, a hundred years later, would lead the fight for Votes for Women. Millicent Garrett Fawcett, who would go on to head the suffragist movement, published a new edition of *Vindication* in 1891 and, in her introduction, Fawcett describes Mary as ahead of her own time, and acknowledges her as the author of the first systematic attack on both inequality and women's lack of political enfranchisement. Thus I feel justified in claiming it was Wollstonecraft who kicked the whole thing off.

Fawcett, together with her older sister Elizabeth Garrett Anderson, was lucky, as was the case for so many women who made their mark on the history of Britain, to have a father who supported her education and her ambitions. Elizabeth became a founder member of the Langham Place Ladies, a group often on my mind as I head for Broadcasting House, around the corner from Langham Place itself. These women, to whom she introduced her little sister, Millicent, would form the foundation of the growing Victorian Women's Movement. Elizabeth became the first woman to qualify as a doctor in Britain, was one of the organisers of the 1866 petition for women's suffrage and had a profound impact on the nineteen-year-old Millicent, who determined to devote her life to the cause.

Two groups with identical aims – women's suffrage – but fundamentally different tactics developed in the late nineteenth century. Millicent Fawcett gathered support across the country, speaking about her suffragist methods of lobbying those powerful men who might be persuaded to change the law in favour of Votes for Women by the strength of logical argument.

Emmeline Pankhurst, whose Women's Social and Political Union would be known as the 'Suffragettes', took a very different approach. The Union was born in Manchester and gained a great deal of support among women across the classes, but Emmeline, who once referred to herself as a hooligan, was too impatient to rely on persuasive argument. Direct action became her favoured form of campaigning.

She was determined no one should be hurt as a result of her 'terrorist' activities, but damaging property was fair game. She even recruited friends such as the composer Ethel Smyth, a keen cricketer with her brothers as a child, to teach other suffragettes the skill of throwing overarm, but with stones and bricks aimed at windows, rather than balls at stumps.

It's impossible to deduce whether it was the suffragette or suffragist movement that achieved the desired end. Both gave up their campaigning activities during the Great War, but the point had been made forcefully to those in power and women's contribution to the war effort could not be ignored when peace came in 1918.

It's generally assumed that Nancy Astor was the first woman to be elected as an MP. She wasn't. That was Constance Markievicz who was one of several women to stand in December 1918. Markievicz was the only one to succeed, but as a Sinn Féin candidate in Dublin she would not take her seat in Westminster. That privilege fell to Nancy Astor a whole year later in December 1919.

My grandmother was born in 1900. She was too young, at the age of only eighteen, to vote in that first election. She often told me how frustrated she felt at being denied 'what should have been my right!' She also talked frequently about the thrill and pride felt ten years later when, at the age of twenty-eight, she was permitted to place her cross on the ballot paper. She never told me which candidate she had supported – 'It's a secret ballot!' she would say.

In her whole life she never missed the chance to use her vote and impressed upon me my duty to exercise the right that had been so hard won. I, too, have never missed an election and I would urge every woman today to read these stories of the women who made it possible for us to be full and equal citizens, and think of them as you head for the polling station. You owe them. Don't waste your vote!

Jenni Murray
February 2018, London

'I do not want them to have
power over men, but over
themselves . . . It is not empire,
but equality and friendship
which women want.'

Mary Wollstonecraft

1

Mary Wollstonecraft

1759–1797

I own a lot of books. If there were a fire in my house, only one would be among the few things that must be saved. Three dogs, a cat, a picture of my family and Mary Wollstonecraft's *A Vindication of the Rights of Woman*. It cost me a ridiculous amount of money and it is not even a first edition. Mine was published in 1796, four years after the first, published in 1792, became a run-away bestseller.

The most precious thing I've ever held in my hands, wearing white gloves in the old

Women's Library when it was housed at the London Metropolitan University in the East End, was one of the rare surviving first editions of this first, truly great feminist manifesto. It's now held in the library at the London School of Economics.

I'm not generally given to a passion for 'things', but holding these books, even my inferior third edition, excites me more than I ever thought possible. They seem to give me a direct connection to a woman who, far ahead of her time, dared to write down just about everything I've ever believed about what used to be assumed was a woman's only lot and, at times, still is. She often seems quite critical of her fellow females, railing at them for being obsessed with romance, clothes and being pretty and pleasing to men. She describes them as 'teeming with capricious fantasies' and says in *A Vindication* that 'all women are to be levelled, by meekness and docility, into one character of yielding softness and gentle compliance'.

In her most critical passage she declares:

> women's giddy minds have only one fixed preoccupation: the desire of establishing themselves . . . by marriage. And this desire

making mere animals of them, when they marry they act as such children may be expected to act – they dress, they paint, and nickname God's creatures. Surely these weak beings are only fit for a seraglio!

She describes marrying for money and security as legal prostitution, but then again she understands the degree to which women are forced into such positions, generally having no rights to an education equal to that enjoyed by boys and rarely an opportunity to earn a living and be financially independent. She does not, in the end, blame women for their own downfall, although she does urge them to drag themselves from the position in which they've been placed. She emphasises that it is not nature but culture that renders women 'weak and wretched'.

'There must,' she writes, 'be more equality established in society, or morality will never gain ground, and this virtuous equality will not rest firmly even when founded on a rock, if one half of mankind be chained to its bottom by fate, for they will be continually undermining it through ignorance or pride.'

Women in the late eighteenth century could assume no rights. Marriage was, for most of them, the best career that could be expected, especially if a husband with a decent amount of money could be found. Once married there was no right for a woman to own a share in property or be protected from domestic violence, and, should a marriage end, the father, not the mother, would be given custody of any children.

There was no right to vote or hold any political office and it was not until 1929 that a case known as the Persons Case, taken by five Canadian women, persuaded the Privy Council in London to agree that a woman should be defined in law as a person. This had not applied in English law before 1929, even though a limited right to vote had been passed by Parliament in 1918 and full suffrage in 1928. It was the Canadian women who won us the right to be defined, like men, as persons. Wollstonecraft's theory that women are made not born would later be echoed by Simone de Beauvoir in *The Second Sex*, published as late as 1949.

Unsurprisingly Wollstonecraft's views were not widely welcomed in her time. Why would men, accustomed to taking a wife as a housemaid, nanny, social secretary and decorative companion, unused to making demands for herself, want things to change? Horace Walpole, the writer, politician and son of the former Prime Minister Sir Robert Walpole, called her 'a hyena in petticoats'.

The second most precious possession on my bookshelves is a first edition, described as 'a new edition', of a book mistakenly entitled *The Rights of Women* – the original was decidedly singular, *Woman*. It was published a hundred years after the original, in 1891, and the introduction was written by one Mrs Henry Fawcett. We now know her rather more correctly as Millicent Garrett Fawcett, one of the leading activists in the suffragist movement (more of her later in the book).

It is clear from Fawcett's glowing approval of Wollstonecraft that her *Vindication* has survived and influenced subsequent generations. Fawcett writes:

Mary Wollstonecraft was ahead of her time and may be regarded, though opinion has moved in the direction in which she pointed, as ahead of ours. In numerous passages she points out the inseparable connection between male and female chastity. One would have thought the fact so self-evident as to need no asseveration; but as a matter of experience we know that even now the mass of people mete out to the two partners in the same action an entirely different degree of blame, and judge them by entirely different standards . . . Against the essential immorality and injustice of this doctrine and practice Mary Wollstonecraft protested with her whole strength. She exposes the insincerity of those who profess zeal for virtue by pointing the finger of scorn at the woman who has transgressed, while her partner who may have tempted her by money, ease, and flattery to her doom, is received with every mark of consideration and respect.

Fawcett goes on:

In one other important respect Mary Wollstonecraft was ahead of her own time in regard to women and in line with the foremost thinkers on this subject in ours. Henrik Ibsen has taken the lead among the moderns in teaching that women have a duty to themselves as well as to their parents, husbands and children, and that truth and freedom are needed for the growth of true womanliness as well as of true manliness . . .

I have already quoted her saying: 'I do not want them to have power over men, but over themselves' . . . 'It is not empire, but equality and friendship which women want' . . . 'Speaking of women at large. *Their first duty is to themselves as rational creatures*' . . . The words italicised foreshadow almost verbatim Nora's expression in the well-known scene in *A Doll's House*, where she tells her astounded husband that she has discovered that she has duties to herself as well as to him and to their children . . . Women need education, need economic independence, need political enfranchisement, need social equality and friendship . . . That woman must choose between being a slave and a queen; 'quickly scorn'd when not ador'd' is a theory of pinch-beck and tinsel . . . Upon this theory, and all that hangs upon it, Mary Wollstonecraft made the first systematic and concentrated attack; and the women's rights movement in England and America owes as much to her as modern Political Economy owes to her famous contemporary, Adam Smith.

Margaret Walters, in her biography of Wollstonecraft, suggests that like the heroine of her first novel (*Mary: A Fiction*, published in 1788), who rejects her parents, Wollstonecraft had 'no models, no one to identify with, so she ha[d], literally to invent herself'. Walters points to the fact that Mary faced the barriers experienced by all women who are determined to exercise their independent minds and suggests it is this all too familiar struggle that gives such a 'curiously modern' quality to her story and explains why we still identify with her so strongly today.

Like so many women who managed to make their way and fulfil 'their first duty to themselves as rational creatures', it was Mary's father who lit what we would now call her feminist light bulb, although in her case, not in a good way. Her family life is a prime example of how the personal becomes political.

She was born in Spitalfields in London in 1759 into a relatively prosperous family. Her paternal grandfather owned a successful silk-weaving business, and when he died in 1765, her father inherited a share of the concern.

With no experience or knowledge of farming

he moved his wife and children to live on a farm in Epping in Essex. Edward Wollstonecraft senior failed at every business he attempted and his daughter Mary would later describe him as a childish bully who abused his wife and family after heavy drinking sessions. She would often intervene to protect her mother from his violence. Elizabeth, her mother, seems to have made no protest on her own behalf.

There were seven Wollstonecraft children – Ned, Mary, Henry Woodstock, Eliza, Everina, James and Charles – and Ned was undoubtedly his mother's favourite. Mary would later write in her novel *Maria: The Wrongs of Woman*, inspired by her mother's adoration of her older brother, 'in comparison with her affection for him, she might be said not to love the rest of her children'.

Of all the children Ned was the only one to receive a 'gentleman's' education, which would prepare him for the Bar. As the family moved around the country from London to Epping, to Yorkshire, back to London, to Wales and finally to London again, the only formal education Mary received was a few years at a day school in Beverley in East Yorkshire where she learned to read and write. From then on everything she learned was self-taught, including several foreign languages.

No wonder such a bright young woman became determined that girls should enjoy the same education as boys. Her hard work and forcefulness did not impress her family, though. She wrote later of her life compared with that of her brother: 'Such indeed is the force of prejudice that what was called spirit and wit in him, was cruelly repressed as forwardness in me.'

There was little opportunity to earn a living for an eighteenth-century middle-class young woman of limited means apart from teaching, becoming a governess, needlework or acting as a lady's companion. Mary tried them all and hated them. Her prospects in the marriage market were poor as there was no money in the family, but then marrying for money would not have fitted her growing political philosophy.

She did attempt to run a girls' school in Newington Green in London in the 1780s. She had rescued her sister Eliza from a brutal marriage and arranged a legal separation for her. They opened the school together in 1784, but it was not a success. Instead she decided to try to become a professional writer.

She was not, as she would describe herself, 'the first of a new genus'. It was not uncommon during this period for women to earn a living by the pen, although the majority were engaged in popular fiction. Mary did not approve, believing the romantic novel to be a dangerous occupation for the young female reading public. Her first work was a stern, moral tract called *Thoughts on the Education of Daughters*, in which she criticised the traditional method of teaching girls, which treated them as inferior to boys. She was delighted to earn £10 from the work and a year later wrote to Eliza, 'I hope you have not forgot that I am an Author.'

It was during her time in Newington Green that she met and befriended a minister, Richard Price. He and a scientist, Joseph Priestley, led a group of intellectuals known as Rational Dissenters. They sought to demystify religion and apply conscience and reason to moral choices. Price became Mary's mentor and, through him, she became acquainted with the leading reformers of the time, including the publisher Joseph Johnson. It was he who commissioned *Thoughts on the Education of Daughters* in 1787. He then published the novel *Mary: A Fiction*, depicting the social limitations oppressing women, and a children's book, *Original Stories from Real Life*. Between 1788 and 1792 she worked for Johnson as a translator and reviewer, helping to found his journal, *Analytical Review*.

Thus she achieved her aim of becoming a pioneer as a liberated woman with the intellectual and financial independence that she advocated for all women. She refused to conform to the demands of high fashion and dressed in a way we would now describe as bohemian. She wore a coarse cloth dress and worsted stockings, wearing her long hair down around her shoulders rather than pinned up as would have been expected of a 'lady'. One disapproving observer described her as 'a philosophical sloven'. She gave up meat and the other 'necessities of life' in order, she said, to better discover the truth of herself. She wrote to one of her women friends, 'Struggle with any obstacles rather than go into a state of dependence . . . I have felt the weight, and would have you by all means avoid it.'

The French Revolution, which began in 1789, became a crucially important event for Mary and her group of liberal intellectuals. She saw it as a struggle for individual liberty against the tyranny of a spoiled and wealthy monarchy and aristocracy. Her friend and mentor, Richard Price, wrote in praise of the revolutionaries and argued that 'the British people, like the French, had the right to remove a bad king from the throne'. He'd earlier been roundly criticised for praising the American Revolution and now the response came from the British statesman Edmund Burke. His heated riposte was called *Reflections on the Revolution in France* and defended the 'inherited rights' of monarchy.

Thomas Paine's response to Burke in 1791, *The Rights of Man*, is probably the better-known work, but Mary was also prompted to respond in support of Price, and of revolution, with a pamphlet entitled 'A Vindication of the Rights of Men', published in 1790. She expressed her opposition to a range of social practices such as the slave trade and addressed human rights and international politics. She also took Burke to task for sympathising with the aristocratic women of France, whom he described as victimised by the Revolution.

'Your tears are reserved,' she wrote, 'very naturally considering your character, for . . . the downfall of queens . . . whilst the distress of many industrious mothers, whose helpmates have been torn from them, and the hungry cry of helpless babes, were vulgar sorrows that could not move your commiseration.'

Her first 'Vindication' was well received by the radicals in London within whom Mary assumed her rightful place, including William Godwin, Samuel Coleridge, Joseph Priestley, William Blake, Thomas Paine and William Wordsworth. These London radicals were exponents of the Enlightenment – the social revolution that celebrated reason as the absolute core of human identity. They sought to redefine the family, the state and education along the lines of the Enlightenment. It was a short step to the aim of sexual equality for Mary to take as she argued women were the moral and intellectual equals of men in her second Vindication – that of 'the Rights of Woman'.

It took her only three months to produce more than three hundred pages and she was not convinced she had done the best possible job. She wrote to a friend, 'I should have written to you sooner had I not been very much engrossed by writing and printing my vindication of the Rights of Woman . . . I shall give the last sheet to the printer today; and,

I am dissatisfied with myself for not having done justice to the subject. Do not suspect me of false modesty – I mean to say, that had I allowed myself more time I could have written a better book.'

Nevertheless, the book had an immediate and positive impact. Lady Palmerston is said to have warned her husband, 'I have been reading the Rights of Woman, so you must in future expect me to be very tenacious of my rights and privileges.' In Glasgow, a Mrs Anne MacVicar Grant wrote that 'the book was so run after here, that there is no keeping it long enough to read it leisurely'.

There were, of course, detractors. The leading evangelical writer and Bluestocking group member Hannah More wrote to Horace Walpole that she had not read the book and found that 'there is something fantastic and absurd in the very title. There is no animal so much indebted to subordination for its good behaviour as woman.' The general opinion of the more conservative women was that the book was an 'Indecent Rhapsody'. One wonders how many of them had actually read it!

Mary was not alone in arguing for women's

as well as men's rights. In the midst of the French Revolution, Olympe de Gouges, correctly arguing that Liberté, Égalité and Fraternité rather left out the female perspective, wrote *Declaration of the Rights of Woman and the Female Citizen*, published in 1791, in which she challenged the exclusion of women from the revolutionaries' *Declaration of the Rights of Man*. She was not so well received as Wollstonecraft. As a result of insisting on women's rights, de Gouges was guillotined on a charge of treason.

Mary's hope that men and women would successfully achieve equality in their education and, consequently, their relationships with each other did not quite work out for her. She had pleaded in *A Vindication* for intellectual companionship to be the ideal of marriage, with women able to be defined by their own character and work rather than by their marriages. When it came to men, she failed to practise what she preached. In London she had fallen passionately in love with a painter and literary figure called Henry Fuseli. He was married and his wife was unaware of their affair. Mary, never one for concealing her feelings, and often more likely to jump into a situation with both feet rather than consider the consequences, decided they should be open about the relationship. She went round to Fuseli's home, asked to see his wife, Sophia, and informed her that the best solution to their dilemma was a ménage à trois. Sophia was furious, thought Mary's plan appalling and threw her out of the house. The affair was over.

In 1792, as her feminist manifesto hit the bookshops, Mary travelled to France, ostensibly to witness the Revolution that had so inspired her, but, rather conveniently, escaping London and the Fuseli scandal. She arrived just as the Jacobin Terror, which would see mass executions and the rise of arbitrary power, was about to begin. Her book, *An Historical and Moral View of the Origin and Progress of the French Revolution*, published in 1794, documents her attempts to reconcile her horror at the violence with her belief in the perfectibility of man. Her disillusionment was profound.

In France, in the midst of political chaos and, as an Englishwoman, great physical danger, Mary lost her heart again. In Paris she was welcomed into a group of British and American free-thinking radicals and, in the early months of 1793, she met Captain Gilbert

Imlay. He was handsome, charming, a former soldier now involved in trade, and Mary fell hopelessly in love.

In November of the same year she wrote to him: 'I have felt some gentle twitches, which make me begin to think, that I am nourishing a creature who will soon be sensible of my care. This thought has . . . produced an overflowing of tenderness to you.'

Imlay did not share her overflowing of tenderness, but he did protect her from the possibility of imprisonment as an Englishwoman as the unrest continued by registering her as his wife at the American Embassy. (They had not actually married.) Americans were protected from the Terror by their nationality, but he soon went off on commercial travels, leaving Mary alone. She followed him to Le Havre, hoping that the birth of their child would bring him closer to her. Fanny was born there in May 1794. Imlay would not become the devoted father Mary had hoped for.

She named her daughter Fanny after her closest friend from childhood, Fanny Blood. William Godwin, in his book about Mary written after her death, said that she and Fanny 'contracted a friendship so fervent as for years to have constituted the ruling passion of her mind'. There is no evidence to suggest that theirs was a sexual relationship, but the two women lived and worked together for ten years and Mary virtually adopted Fanny's family as her own.

In 1785 Fanny had travelled to Lisbon to marry an Irishman who lived there. She became pregnant and Mary went to Lisbon to be with her at the time of the birth. Fanny died in childbirth and Godwin wrote that Mary had named her daughter Fanny after 'the dear friend of her youth, whose image could never be erased from her memory'.

After her daughter's birth, Mary followed Imlay to London where she hoped they would set up a family home together. He was busy with his commercial ventures, beginning to see other women and had no interest in family life. Mary made her first attempt at suicide by taking an overdose of opium, but was found and revived by a maid.

The miserable relationship dragged on. It seems astonishing that such a rational, clever woman could have allowed herself to be used and abused by such a man, but, when he asked her to go to Norway to sort out a

JENNI MURRAY

business problem for him she packed her bag and, with her tiny baby and a maid, set out for Scandinavia. She spent several months negotiating for compensation for a cargo of Imlay's that had been stolen by the Norwegian captain of his ship.

When she returned to London she was told by her cook that Imlay had another new mistress – an actress – and Mary made her second attempt at suicide. She walked to Putney Bridge and threw herself into the River Thames, but was rescued by two passing boatmen. Still she tried to revive the relationship with Imlay, constantly pleading for reconciliation. She gave up hope in 1796 when she wrote her last letter to him. 'I now solemnly assure you this is an eternal farewell . . . I part with you in peace.'

When Mary had first met William Godwin, the author of *An Enquiry Concerning Political Justice*, and one of the leading radicals of the time, it had been at a dinner party at Joseph Johnson's house in 1791. The two had argued about religion and appeared to dislike each other. But then, in 1796, soon after she ended her relationship with Imlay, Mary made the first move on Godwin – not the sort of thing expected of a late-eighteenth-century woman! She went to his house, ostensibly to lend him a book, and they quickly began a highly charged erotic relationship.

Mary's letters to Godwin bubble with obvious delight at their physical passion for each other. In November 1796 she wrote to him, 'If the felicity of last night has had the same effect on your health as on my countenance, you have no cause to lament your failure of resolution for I have seldom seen so much live fire running about my features as this morning when recollections – very dear; called forth the blush of pleasure, as I adjusted my hair.'

Wollstonecraft and Godwin did not intend to marry – both had political reservations about the marital state and it was generally assumed, as Mary continued to use the name Imlay, that she had been married in Paris. But early in 1797 Mary discovered she was pregnant and the two decided to wed, causing yet another scandal as so many of their friends had assumed she was already married. A number dropped her, shocked that Fanny had been born out of wedlock.

Mary and Godwin seem to have achieved the

kind of marriage she had hoped for. She moved into his house in Somers Town in London and he rented a study for use during the day. They wrote and visited friends, often separately, as both were keen to retain their independence, and Mary looked forward to the arrival of the child she called, in advance of 'his' arrival, 'little William'.

She gave birth on 30 August to Mary – later Shelley and the author of *Frankenstein* – but the placenta had to be removed manually by the midwife, causing the puerperal fever from which she died eleven days after her labour.

Godwin wrote to a friend that he believed he would never find happiness again, but he did manage to write a memoir of his wife only two years after her death in which he detailed her sexual exploits. It did nothing to enhance her reputation, but no doubt made him and the two girls a pretty penny. Life, as they say, is copy.

The memoir led to some condemnation of Wollstonecraft, notably by the nineteenth-century sociologist Harriet Martineau, who wrote:

Women who would improve the condition and chances of their sex must, I am certain, be not only affectionate and devoted, but rational and dispassionate . . . But Mary Wollstonecraft was, with all her powers, a poor victim of passion, with no control over her own peace, and no calmness or content except when the needs of her individual nature were satisfied.

Later in the nineteenth century, as we have seen, she was championed as an exponent of total equality between the sexes by suffragists and educationalists such as Millicent Garrett Fawcett and Barbara Bodichon and, by the twentieth century, as attitudes to sex became more liberal, she had become the feminist hero she is today. Virginia Woolf summed up her impact:

She whose sense of her own existence was so intense, who had cried out even in her misery, 'I cannot bear to think of being no more – of losing myself – nay, it appears to be impossible that I should cease to exist,' died at the age of thirty-six [*sic*; she was thirty-eight]. But she has her revenge. Many millions have died and been forgotten in the hundred and thirty years that have passed since she was buried; and yet as we read her letters and listen to her arguments and consider her experiments, above all, that most fruitful experiment, her relation with Godwin, and realise the high-handed and hot-blooded manner in which she cut her way to the quick of life, one form of immortality is hers undoubtedly; she is alive and active, she argues and experiments, we hear her voice and trace her influence even now among the living.

'The first thing women must
learn is to dress like ladies and
behave like gentlemen.'

Elizabeth Garrett Anderson

2

Elizabeth Garrett Anderson

1836–1917

As far as medicine goes, I've chosen Elizabeth Garrett Anderson as the first woman to qualify as a medical doctor in Britain because she did so as a woman, went on to specialise in women and children, and worked hard for the greater emancipation of women throughout her long life.

She was not, though, strictly the first. James Miranda Stuart Barry, who is thought to have entered this world in 1789 and lived until 1865, was actually born Margaret Anne Bulkley and qualified more than fifty years before Garrett

Anderson. Bulkley chose to disguise herself as a man in order to gain acceptance to the medical school in Edinburgh. She lived the rest of her life as a man, working as a military surgeon, serving in India and in Cape Town, South Africa, where there is a museum dedicated to her/his achievements, one of which was the first Caesarean carried out in Africa where both the mother and child survived.

Barry died in England from dysentery and the woman who cared for him and dealt with the body reported to the authorities, after the funeral, that she had examined his anatomy and that she had discovered Inspector General Dr James Barry to be, in fact, female, and the stretch marks on his stomach indicated that he had, at some time, given birth to a child. The subterfuge came to light in an exchange of letters between George Graham of the General Register Office and Major D. R. McKinnon, the doctor who had issued the death certificate on which Barry was identified as male.

McKinnon in his letter said that it was none of his business whether Dr Barry was a male or a female. He said he could only positively swear that the identity of the body was that of a person with whom he had been acquainted as

Inspector General of Hospitals for a period of years. She certainly deserves an acknowledgement here.

Elizabeth Garrett was born in Whitechapel in London and was the second of the nine children of Newson Garrett and his wife, Louisa. The family became well-to-do as the children grew up. Garrett was a self-made man who started out as a pawnbroker and developed a business as a grain merchant and maltster, operating out of Aldeburgh in Suffolk, which is where Elizabeth spent most of her childhood.

She was educated by her mother, then by a governess at home before attending, for five years from 1849, a boarding school for ladies at Blackheath in Kent run by the aunts of the poet Robert Browning. It was during this period that she met Emily Davies, who would later found Girton College, the first Cambridge college for women. The two of them became active members of the Langham Place circle and agreed on the careers they would pursue as part of their determined campaign to forward the advancement of women's rights and professional opportunities. Garrett would open the medical profession to women and

Davies planned to open the doors of British universities.

The Langham Place Ladies were a group of middle-class, highly educated women who were associated with the Society for Promoting the Employment of Women and the *English Woman's Journal*. I think of them often when I arrive for work at Broadcasting House, around the corner from Langham Place. They were the foundation of the growing Victorian women's movement. As a result of her activities with the 'ladies' Garrett met Dr Elizabeth Blackwell, an Englishwoman who had been raised in the United States where she had, despite endless barriers placed in her way, managed to study medicine and obtain a degree.

Blackwell had come to London to have her name entered on the General Medical Council's newly established register. There was a temporary provision for doctors who qualified overseas to be registered after the Medical Act of 1858 and Blackwell was then, for a short time, the only woman on the list. During her visit she promoted the cause of women who wanted to enter the medical profession. Garrett was inspired.

Her father took some persuading that this

was a suitable plan for a daughter of his. Mr Garrett had been a supporter of the education of his girls, but he was also a man deeply steeped in Victorian values. A respectable daughter with a good marriage was the aim of every responsible father, and the thought of his girl being involved in work that would have involved blood, guts and the more intimate parts of the human anatomy must have horrified him.

With Blackwell's support, Elizabeth managed to win him round to the extent that he agreed to give her his full support with both connections and finance. She was then able to begin her attempts to overcome the difficulties of prejudice against women she knew she would face. The profession was entirely dominated by men who, like her father, would have found the idea of a woman wielding a scalpel or discussing personal matters with a sick patient utterly unacceptable.

She made formal applications to several London teaching hospitals and to Edinburgh and St Andrews. She was turned down as a student by all of them, although Middlesex Hospital offered her a trial period from 1860 to 1861. She was to work as a nurse, but be given access to the operating theatre and classes on materia medica (medicine), Latin and Greek with the hospital's apothecary.

Eventually she was allowed into the dissecting room, but this seems to have proved too much for her shocked male colleagues. In 1861 they presented a memo to the hospital's medical school authorities making clear their determination that a woman should not be allowed admittance as a fellow student. They argued that the work they were expected to do with patients, cadavers and in the laboratory was simply not suitable for feminine sensibilities. Elizabeth was also an attractive young woman, modestly dressed in the style of the day with her hair neatly tied up in a bun, but her erstwhile colleagues were not happy with the distraction that the female of the species presented. What's more likely is that they were jealous of her academic and practical abilities.

The hospital excluded her from any further study there. But this was a woman who was described in her youth as being of indomitable will, unprepared to suffer fools gladly. She threatened legal action and the Society of Apothecaries, responsible for issuing medical licences, acknowledged that they could not prevent her from taking their examinations as long as she completed the required courses of study. This she had to do as a private student of teachers from recognised medical schools and after serving an apprenticeship under a licensed apothecary.

Happily, her wealthy, determined and by now encouraging father financed her and, in 1865, she obtained the licence of the Society of Apothecaries, which entitled her to have her name on the medical register. Only three of the seven applicants who took the exam passed it and Elizabeth gained the top marks. No wonder those young men were jealous and resentful. Soon after, the Society decided that no more women would be allowed to register, so Elizabeth was the first woman qualified in Britain to achieve such official status and the last until the Medical Act of 1876 allowed the British medical authorities to license all qualified applicants, regardless of gender.

In order to become a fully qualified doctor she had to leave the country and study at the University of Paris, and her low-status qualification as an apothecary was now raised to the level of MD. She was the first woman to achieve the degree, and in 1873 she was admitted to membership of the British Medical Association. In 1878 pressure was put on her to resign her membership as the BMA had voted against the admission of any more women. She refused and was the only female member for the next nineteen years, just one of several cases where Garrett would be the first woman to enter an all-male medical institution which would then block any further applications by women.

Now she was fully qualified to work as a doctor, Garrett set up her own practice in Upper Berkeley Street in London, just around the corner from fashionable Harley Street and only a few minutes' walk from Langham Place where the 'ladies' had congregated. She also set up the St Mary's Dispensary for Women and Children in Marylebone and, for this project, being well-connected among London's wealthy proved a great help. Charitable funds were found for the dispensary itself, as well as money to pay the fees for women who could not afford their own treatment.

Elizabeth had, for obvious reasons, a keen interest in education and in 1870 she stood as a candidate for the London School Board, the first time women had been allowed to stand. Robert Browning was an active supporter, as were a number of husbands of her more wealthy and influential patients. She won the highest number of votes in the whole of the capital.

James George Skelton Anderson was chairman of her election campaign. He worked for the Orient Steamship Line and was a son of a clergyman. The two married in 1871 and she went on to have three children, first a son, Alan, and two daughters, Margaret and Louisa. Margaret died of meningitis in 1875. All her children had the name Garrett Anderson, the name by which Elizabeth was known after her marriage. It was a rare move in the period for a married woman to insist that her own family name should continue down her line. Her younger sister, Millicent Garrett, a leading suffragist, did the same thing, becoming Millicent Garrett Fawcett – more of her in the next chapter.

Elizabeth carried on working hard after marriage and motherhood, becoming a model for the mother who also wants to have a career, although she did resign an honorary post at the East London Hospital for Children, which she'd held since 1870, and she quit the school board. I guess even with the funds to pay for adequate childcare it wasn't absolutely possible to have it all! She once said, 'A doctor leads two lives, the professional and the private, and the boundaries between the two are never traversed.'

Her creation of the first hospital dedicated to the health of women with only female medical staff to care for them occurred in 1871, the same year as her wedding. The New Hospital for Women began as just ten beds above the dispensary, and the doctors she appointed were unregistered as they had medical degrees obtained abroad.

It was around this time that Elizabeth began to enter into the political arena on behalf of the burgeoning feminist movement. In 1874 Henry Maudsley (now known for his hospital in south London and his work in mental health) wrote an article on 'Sex and Mind in Education' in which he argued that education for women caused overexertion, and thus reduced their reproductive capacity, sometimes causing 'nervous and even mental disorders'. Elizabeth countered his argument by saying the real danger to women's mental health was not their education, but boredom. She said fresh air and exercise were infinitely preferable to sitting by the fire reading a novel.

It was in the same year, 1874, that she became a joint founder of the London School of Medicine for Women together with another medical pioneer, Sophia Jex-Blake. Elizabeth became a lecturer in the only medical school available to women and was Dean of the school from 1883 to 1902. She gave her students access to patients in the hospital, set them an example of female professionalism and always told them that 'the first thing women must learn is to dress like ladies and behave like gentlemen'. The school was later renamed the Royal Free Hospital of Medicine and prepared students for London University's medical degree, which was open to women from 1878.

In 1872 the New Hospital for Women moved to larger premises and then, in 1874, to a purpose-built facility on Euston Road. In 1918, the year after her death, it was named the Elizabeth Garrett Anderson and Obstetric Hospital and continued to employ only women doctors until it was absorbed into University College Hospital in the 1980s. It had been under threat of complete closure since the

1960s, but, when closure was announced by Camden Health Authority, the building was occupied in protest by the staff. The campaign to keep the hospital open continued until 1979. There is still an Elizabeth Garrett Anderson wing at UCH's new building, serving maternity and neonatal cases since 2008, but both male and female medical staff are employed.

By 1880 Garrett Anderson had set up a successful private practice alongside her work for poorer women and, in insisting that she would have only women caring for other women, she was able to conform to some degree to those Victorian standards of modesty that had threatened to block her advancement earlier in her career. Mind you, even today there are lots of women who would prefer to deal with a doctor of their own sex, particularly if their medical problems are obstetric or gynaecological. I remember a great sense of disappointment among my acquaintances – all in the midst of our childbearing years – when the principle she had established of women treating women was lost.

In addition to her clinical work, Garrett Anderson also became a surgeon – unusual for a woman even today – much to the horror of the management board of the hospital, who refused to allow major surgery to be performed on the premises. She went ahead and success-fully removed a patient's diseased ovary – a very dangerous operation at the time. She wrote a short medical textbook, *The Student's Pocket Index*, in 1878, sharing the experience that she felt needed to be passed on to other young women entering the profession. She also contributed numerous articles on cases to the *British Medical Journal* and wrote for newspapers on medical matters and the women's cause.

In 1902, after a phenomenally successful career, Elizabeth and her husband moved back to the Garrett family home in Aldeburgh after the death of her mother. Her husband died five years later after suffering a stroke. She was pretty much retired from her medical work – she had resigned as senior physician at the New Hospital in 1892, only remaining as a consultant, but she did stand as mayor of Aldeburgh in 1908 and was elected. Thus she achieved another first – no other woman had ever succeeded in becoming a mayor in Britain.

Her two-year stint as mayor gave her an opportunity to pursue her interests in housing and sanitation, knowing that one of the most vital ways of improving the health of the population was to ensure that there was a substantial roof over the head of every family and that cleanliness would help keep infection and disease at bay. She was also a prime mover in the women's suffrage movement. She had begun her campaigning for women to have the vote in 1866 when she and Emily Davies gathered more than 1,500 signatures on a petition asking that female heads of households should have the right to vote. She joined the first British Women's Suffrage Committee and became a member, in 1889, of the Central Committee of the National Society for Women's Suffrage.

After her husband's death, Elizabeth became even more active. She shocked some of Aldeburgh's town councillors by becoming, in 1908, a supporter of Emmeline Pankhurst's Women's Social and Political Union (WSPU), the more radical wing of the campaign, although in 1912 she stepped back from women who believed active revolution was the best way forward and publicly rejected the militant tactics of the suffragettes. She now leaned towards the suffragists' approach, led by her sister, Millicent Garrett Fawcett, believing that lobbying powerful men might be more effective. It was, in reality, an approach more suited to her character, which had always employed research, information and reasoned argument, rather than breaking windows or tying oneself to the railings of Parliament. Her daughter Louisa, on the other hand, who also became a doctor, joined the militant suffragettes and was imprisoned in 1912 for her activities.

Dr Elizabeth Garrett Anderson died in 1917 after a long illness and was consequently denied the opportunity of ever marking a ballot paper with a cross. The Great War was coming to a close and the following year, 1918, would see the Representation of the People Act in which limited suffrage was won for women of property over the age of thirty. It would take another ten years for universal suffrage to be achieved for all men and women over the age of twenty-one in the Equal Franchise Act of 1928.

Elizabeth is buried in the churchyard of St Peter and St Paul's Church in Aldeburgh, and I just wish I could tell her that now fifty-eight per cent of all doctors in training are female. They have a great deal for which to thank her.

'I cannot say I became a suffragist.
I always was one, from the time I
was old enough to think at all
about the principles of
Representative Government.'

Millicent Garrett Fawcett

3

Millicent Garrett Fawcett

1847–1929

I've often wondered whether, had I been around before women won the vote, I would have been a militant suffragette or a suffragist, relying on my capacity for reasoned argument and lobbying those powerful men in Parliament whose support would be necessary to get the law changed. Although I've been the President of the Fawcett Society – now the only organisation in Britain to work consistently for equality between men and women – since 2003, I suspect I may have been so angry and anxious for a speedy fulfilment of the demand for No Taxation without Representation that I may well have smashed a window or two, burned a post box and chained myself to the railings.

That was not Millicent Fawcett's way. Like her sister Elizabeth she spent her childhood in Aldeburgh in Suffolk, where she had been born. The Garretts were a close and loving family where the children were encouraged to learn, get plenty of physical exercise, read and sit around the dinner table for conversation and discussion. Their father, Newson, had been a Conservative politically, but he became a convert to Liberalism and the family was fervently interested in political debate.

Like her older sister, Milly attended the school in Blackheath, Kent from eleven, leaving at fifteen with a passion for literature, the arts and further education. Through Elizabeth and Louisa, the older sister who died young at the age of only thirty-two, she got to know the Langham Place Ladies and learned about the embryonic women's movement and its supporters.

She heard John Stuart Mill speak and was present when Garrett Anderson and Emily Davies organised the 1866 petition for women's suffrage. It called for 'the representation of all householders, without distinction of sex, who possess such property or rental qualifications as your honourable House may determine'. The two older women would not allow her to sign it. At the age of only nineteen they considered her too young, but they made no objection to her expending a huge amount of energy persuading others to sign it. There were 1,499 signatures on the petition when it was presented to Parliament by Mill. It failed.

It was, though, the start of Millicent's lifelong devotion to the cause of winning the vote for women. She was supported and encouraged by the friends she met through her sister and, of course, Elizabeth's struggles to qualify as a doctor naturally fired her little sister's enthusiasm for emancipation. It's said that, even as a teenager, Milly was identified as a possible leader of the suffrage movement and she later said of herself, 'I cannot say I became a suffragist. I always was one, from the time I was old enough to think at all about the principles of Representative Government.'

Milly married very young. She was eighteen when she met Henry Fawcett at a party held by a group of keen suffragists, and they married two years later. He was fourteen years her senior, a Professor of Political Economy at Cambridge and a Liberal MP. He had been with John Stuart Mill when the 1866 petition was presented to Parliament.

Millicent Fawcett described their marriage as having 'perfect intellectual sympathy'. They shared their politics, also had compatible interests in walking, rowing, riding and skating, and shared a sense of humour. A year after their marriage their first and only child, Philippa, was born.

The marriage was an extremely happy one. Henry was blind and, as Millicent acted as her husband's eyes, he was able to open political doors for her, introducing her to the men she would need to lobby if her aims were to be achieved. Henry supported her completely. Without such a sympathetic husband she would not have been able to run their houses in Cambridge and London, care for a new baby, write articles, act as his secretary, speak in public for the suffragist cause and be an active member of the Women's Suffrage Committee.

Henry Fawcett encouraged his wife to write, in addition to all her other activities. She managed to pen two novels, publish two works on classical economics and write the introduction to a new edition of Mary Wollstonecraft's great work, *A Vindication of the Rights of Woman*, although the Victorian version slipped up and replaced 'Woman' with 'Women'! I've never quite understood why such an active campaigner for women, on the cover of the new edition, is named as Mrs Henry Fawcett. It was the common way to address a married woman at the time, but one she rarely used. She was always Millicent Garrett Fawcett.

Being at the forefront of a controversial national campaign was not a recipe for an easy life. I haven't seen pictures of Milly wearing anything but a traditional Victorian woman's outfit with a high neck and full skirt. But she was leading a revolution where women walked the streets or rode their bicycles (shock, horror!) in the new-fangled 'Rational Dress', which allowed some ease of movement and less corseted restriction. Some women were even courageous enough to wear a banner demanding 'Votes for Women' across the chest.

Punch cartoonists had a field day. They began to publish a torrent of abusive cartoons lampooning the suffrage cause; the magazine seemed to represent the view not only of comic artists and politicians but the majority of the British public as well. Millicent made lots of attempts to avert disapproval by her respectable behaviour and her clever, well-informed speeches, and she steadfastly refused to be put off by the widely held view that achieving the aims of the women's movement would be fraught with difficulties and would take a very long time. She chose to dismiss the strength of the opposition they faced and never wavered in her determination to promote the cause.

In 1997 Shelagh Diplock, a former director of the Fawcett Society, described Millicent as a formidable, if never a particularly charismatic, speaker:

Millicent Garrett Fawcett, at the age of twenty-two, set out on the first speaking tour of her sixty-year-long campaign for women's suffrage. She would list the many reasons given why women should not be given the vote. It was said that women were intellectually inferior. They were physically inferior. They were too pure to be involved in politics. If given the vote, they would neglect their families and homes. Men would no longer open doors for them. Women did not really want the vote and so on. Then, one by one, she would demolish these points using her sharp logical mind and quick wit. This powerful mix of reasoned arguments to promote a cause, combined with humour to keep an audience listening, remains a most effective strategy to this day.

The Women's Suffrage Committee soon became the London Society for Women's Suffrage as other groups around the country, in Edinburgh and Manchester, began to be formed. They had all been heartened by the fact that Millicent's petition had at least been seen in Parliament: 'For the first step forward had been taken, the challenge had been thrown down, and the Cause had been advanced into the political lists.' But their belief that the cause would be popular simply because it was just was misguided.

Nevertheless, the movement grew. There were numerous strong and resourceful women who were prepared to endure the ridicule they faced in standing up for women's rights, and there were a number of men who also proved essential to the movement. Always positioned at the front of her armies of supporters was Millicent Garrett Fawcett. She served on the board of most of the suffrage organisations, spoke on platforms, wrote and lobbied.

There were endless difficulties and debates about where the women's campaigning energies should be concentrated. As we've seen in the previous chapter, medicine and education were the preoccupations of Elizabeth Garrett Anderson and Emily Davies, but for young Millicent, the vote was the main focus and she was continually aware of the need to avoid the racier side of the campaign and remain the calm, informed lobbyist who had to persuade rather than alienate the powerful men whose minds she wanted to change.

As a consequence of the need to present a respectable front, Milly was forced to back down from a campaign she would have dearly loved to support. Josephine Butler was a fellow feminist and social reformer who, between 1869 and 1886, worked to have the Contagious Diseases Act repealed. The Act required that any woman suspected of being a prostitute must be examined for venereal infection. If she were found to have the disease she would be locked in hospital until she was cured. If she refused to submit to a genital examination she could be given a prison sentence of up to three months.

Milly agreed with Butler that it was unjust that prostitutes, or indeed any woman suspected or accused of being one, should be examined regularly for venereal disease when the men who bought their bodies were not subjected to such demands. But Butler's efforts were widely considered unsuitable for a woman of modest Victorian conduct. Millicent was keen that she should not be associated with the 'violent opposition' the Butler campaign aroused and supported her only in private.

As the century wore on and further attempts were made by sympathetic MPs to bring forward a Bill or resolution to advance the cause of suffrage, the tone of the response in the House was said to be not so much hostile as facetious. The women's reasoned arguments and demands were simply not taken seriously, even in Parliament.

In 1884 Henry Fawcett died suddenly, leaving Millicent a widow at the age of only thirty-seven. Her naturally reticent nature prevented any outpouring of emotion, but those close to her commented on how deeply she grieved for him. She never considered marrying again.

Millicent sold the houses in Cambridge and London and moved with Philippa and one of her sisters, Agnes, into 2 Gower Street in Bloomsbury, where a blue plaque now honours her memory. She was not short of money. Her sister was a successful businesswoman who ran a home improvement company and Millicent made a living from her writing. She made regular contributions to the *Contemporary Review* and wrote a number of biographies, including *Some Eminent Women of Our Times* and *The Life of Her Majesty Queen Victoria*.

She also became the suffrage movement's official leader, becoming the president in 1897 of the National Union of Women's Suffrage Societies (NUWSS) and adopting the suffragist colours of green, white and red (GWR) – the initials stood for 'Give Women Rights', and differed from the suffragettes' green, white and purple, symbolising hope, purity and dignity.

Not all of her views would play well with modern members of the society named after her, which, in 2016, celebrated its one hundred and fiftieth anniversary – the history of the Fawcett Society began at the time of the 1866 petition to Parliament presented by John Stuart Mill and Henry Fawcett.

Millicent supported compulsory primary education for young children, but believed parents should be expected to pay for it and be prevented from profiting from the earnings of their young. As a believer in the principle of family responsibility she opposed free school meals and later family allowances, and she was active in an unpopular campaign in the late 1880s for children to be banned from working in pantomime or in the theatre.

As a passionate believer in the free market, she had been a supporter of the National Union of Working Women and was concerned about the welfare of working-class women, but she did not approve of legislation to protect them. She felt that there should be no discriminatory legislation on the part of women that was not equally available to men.

She even caused controversy and was widely opposed when she questioned the case for intervention on the part of women whose faces had been horribly mutilated during the course of their work at Bryant and May's match factory in the East End of London. The condition was known as 'phossy jaw', as the necrosis was caused by the phosphorus used to make the matches. The social activist Annie Besant published an exposé in the magazine *The Link* describing the factory as a prison house and the girls as white slaves.

Besant encouraged and supported the girls during the Match Girls' Strike of 1888, which became an extremely significant moment in the history of the trade union movement. Bad employers were shamed in the press, the match girls, aided by Annie Besant, forced Bryant and May to agree to improve their conditions and a union, one of the first to represent women and a then rare example of a union for unskilled workers, was formed and would last until 1903. *The Link* described the strike as putting 'new heart into all who are struggling for liberty and justice'.

Millicent was aware of how badly women workers were paid compared to men and her major contribution to economic theory was an analysis of the inequality of women's wages. She wrote that it was an inevitable consequence of two things: the 'crowding' of women into a narrow range of jobs as a result of laws that restricted women's opportunities for employment, and discrimination against women perpetrated by the male trade union movement. She argued that it was counterproductive for women to demand equal pay for equal work because the labour market made it impossible for them to achieve equal work – an argument that's common even today when the fight for equal opportunity and equal pay goes on.

Millicent thought demanding more money might well persuade employers that it was hardly worth employing women at all if they ceased to be the cheaper option. She abandoned that argument when the range of jobs open to women was widened during the First World War, as men went to the front and women took up the jobs they had left behind to keep the country working.

In some ways, then, she was a rebel against her times, but she was also a woman of her time. She had statesmanlike qualities, which made her an important leader of the British women's movement, but her Victorian values are clear. She was a passionate believer in the British Empire and a severe opponent of Home Rule for Ireland and independence for India. She also became closely associated with the purity movement, prompted by the exposure of child prostitution by the newspaper editor W. T. Stead, who was a pioneer of investigative journalism. He arranged the purchase of a thirteen-year-old girl, Eliza Armstrong, to highlight the existence of the trade, and wrote a series of devastating articles about child exploitation in the *Pall Mall Gazette*. He was later imprisoned for three months, having been found guilty of failing to secure the permission of the girl's father for the purchase. The story inspired George Bernard Shaw to write *Pygmalion* and call his character Eliza.

Millicent was one of a number of women who joined the purity movement as a result and she campaigned for years, as a founder member of the National Vigilance Association, to protect girls from being trapped into prostitution, to curb child abuse by raising the age of consent, to make incest a criminal offence, to stamp out the 'white slave trade' and to make cruelty to children within the family illegal. She had some success. One of her most vociferous campaigns was to end the practice of excluding women from courtrooms when sexual offences were being considered.

She did tend to be rather censorious in a way that might not appeal to modern feminists, although she did, at least, insist that equality should dominate her moral arguments. By her moral code, neither men nor women were suitable for public office if they indulged in private immorality. She disapproved publicly of a friend who became pregnant before marriage and she tried to destroy the career of the Unionist MP Harry Cust. He was an unrepentant seducer, which, for Millicent, overrode his strong support for the suffragist cause. When some Edwardian feminists began to advocate 'free love' she was appalled and a copy of the *Freewoman*, which was sent to her, was torn up into small pieces and described as 'objectionable and mischievous'. So perhaps it's surprising that, when she gave evidence to the Gorell Commission on divorce in 1910, she argued in favour of divorce by consent.

As Britain moved into a new century, mass support for women's suffrage grew and even the passionately non-violent Millicent had to acknowledge that it was the militant campaign launched by the Pankhursts in 1905 that had really brought the movement to the attention of the nation. As the nineteenth century had come to a close, the NUWSS seemed to have made little progress towards the goal of winning votes for women. Letters of congratulation had been dispatched to their sisters in places like Australia and Wyoming, where women had achieved what the British campaigners had failed so spectacularly to win.

The National Union of Women's Suffrage Societies was reorganised under Millicent's presidency in 1907 and was by far the largest of the suffrage societies with more than fifty thousand members by 1913. It remained committed to constitutional reform. Through her close connections with the universities she attracted well-educated women into the leadership of the movement, which helped give credibility to the cause among educated men. She arranged demonstrations and marches in which she took the lead and in 1908 became the first woman to address the Oxford Union, although the Union did not vote in favour of votes for women until 1913.

Millicent worked hard to attract working-class women into the movement, to join the educated women who had already signed up, saying she believed in 'a grand freemasonry between different classes of women'. It's been suggested by the historian Janet Howarth that the law-abiding strategy of the NUWSS was more popular among working women than suffragette militancy.

As the direct action policy of the Pankhursts' WSPU stepped up there was growing tension between the suffragists and suffragettes. Millicent described this period as 'the most difficult time of my forty years of suffrage work'. She openly expressed her disapproval of the suffragettes' storming of Parliament in 1909, describing it as an 'immoral and dastardly thing to have done'. She was, though, determined that no war should be declared between the suffragists and the suffragettes. The individual suffragettes who made the headlines and were courageous enough to face imprisonment, hunger strikes and force-feeding won her admiration. In 1906 she had held a banquet at the Savoy in honour of the first ten suffragette prisoners, although she was criticised for it in the press and by those who considered the suffragettes' violent tactics to be illegal acts that deserved severe punishment.

The two sides of the movement split in 1912, when the acts of symbolic violence such as breaking windows escalated into arson and bombings. The suffragettes never killed or even injured anyone, but it was clear to Millicent that such acts were damaging to the cause. Still, she argued that the government was responsible for provoking women into breaking the law, while also declaring that the punishments meted out to them, such as long prison sentences and force-feeding, were excessive given the nature of their crimes. The tariff for length of sentence was, she said, more lenient for men, even if their crimes had been more heinous.

The First World War brought an end to activism in the suffrage cause, but Millicent held the NUWSS together by directing its members into war work and was admired by a wide range of politicians for her efforts. There were, though, some serious fallings-out with fellow suffragists who, conflating feminism with pacifism, objected to her wholehearted, patriotic support for the war effort. She saw the war as a necessary conflict that was defending free institutions against the militarism of Prussia.

In 1917 it became accepted that the franchise should be granted to all servicemen, which effectively meant universal suffrage for all adult males. Before the war only men over twenty-one who owned property had the right to vote.

The 1918 Representation of the People Act extended the right to all men over twenty-one, regardless of wealth or class. An all-party speakers' conference held in 1917 was persuaded to recommend a limited right to vote for women.

There's no doubt the war and women's work in nursing, running the railways, driving ambulances and working in factories certainly contributed to the change of mind, but it's clear that pressure from Millicent, particularly in persuading Lloyd George to support her, was instrumental in the fight being won. She also persuaded her members to compromise and accept the limited enfranchisement on offer in 1918. She lobbied politicians to ensure the Bill passed through Parliament in 1918 and women over the age of thirty who owned property won the first step towards universal suffrage, which was finally achieved ten years later in 1928.

Millicent was now seventy-one and gave old age as her reason for resigning from the presidency of the NUWSS in 1919. It was rechristened the National Union of Societies for Equal Citizenship (NUSEC) and she remained associated with it for the last decade of her life. She was a vice president of the League of

Nations Union, took part in campaigns to open up the legal profession and the civil service to women, fought for women to have equal access to divorce and continued to argue for equal suffrage.

During the Paris peace conference, she led a deputation that hoped to place women's suffrage on the agenda, and she was persuaded, as a result of women's war work, to begin to press for equal pay. She was, though, never persuaded by feminist contemporaries such as Eleanor Rathbone that family allowance was a good thing. She resigned from the NUSEC in 1925 when the union voted to press for family allowance. She never changed her attitudes to morality and imperialism, although she did say she approved of the change of fashion after the war, which freed women from restrictive corsets and shortened their skirts and their hair.

Millicent Garrett Fawcett has, I believe, been grossly underestimated in the story of the battle for votes for women. She was the most tireless campaigner for women to have equal rights as citizens and fought for us to have the right to education, work and freedom from exploitation and sexual abuse. In 1925 her efforts were recognised when she became

Dame Millicent Garrett Fawcett. At the end of a long career, during which she never stopped working for her causes, she died after a short illness at her home in Gower Street in 1929. She was cremated at Golders Green and her memorial in Westminster Abbey, added in 1932 to the monument to her husband, says: 'She won citizenship for Women.'

'I am what you call a hooligan.'

Emmeline Pankhurst

4

Emmeline Pankhurst

1858–1929

It's Emmeline Pankhurst's name that has long been most closely associated with the campaign for votes for women, although, I hope, after the preceding chapter on Millicent Garrett Fawcett, it will become clear that it was both the peaceful and persuasive suffragist movement combined with the militant, publicity-conscious tactics of Pankhurst's suffragettes that made the cause impossible to ignore.

Emmeline Pankhurst was born in Sloane Street in Moss Side, Manchester to Robert Goulden, who owned a calico printing and bleach works, and his wife, Sophia Jane Craine. I've always found it deliciously ironic that her mother was born on the Isle of Man. Emmeline was the eldest of ten children and, from an early age, had to do her bit to care for her younger siblings.

She was educated at home, learned to read when she was very young and it was her job to read the daily paper to her father while he ate his breakfast. An interest in politics was thus fostered at the table. Family history also taught her that protest was a necessary part of politics if you felt something passionately. Her paternal grandfather had taken part in the Peterloo demonstration for parliamentary reform and universal suffrage in 1819. A huge crowd of demonstrators gathered peacefully in what's now St Peter's Square in Manchester – between sixty and eighty thousand – and were set upon by a cavalry charge. Sabres were drawn and civilian blood shed in a defining moment of British history. The number killed is not altogether clear. Some sources say fifteen, others eighteen, but it's agreed that at least one woman and a child were among them. Some were killed by sabres, others by clubs or by being trampled to death by the horses. Some seven hundred lay injured. It became known as the Peterloo Massacre and so shocked a local businessman, John Edward Taylor, that he went on to help set up the *Manchester Guardian* newspaper. Mr Goulden senior was said to have narrowly missed death.

Emmeline's brothers called her 'the diction- ary' because she had such a command of the English language. She spoke well, wrote well and they envied her perfect spelling. She is said to have been in bed one night, pretending to be asleep, when she heard her father say, 'What a pity she wasn't born a lad.'

She had learned for herself that girls' edu- cation was considered less important than that of boys when she was sent with her sister to a middle-class girls' school. She was appalled when she found little emphasis on reading, writing, arithmetic or any kind of intellectual pursuit there. A lot of her lessons were devoted to learning how to be the perfect housewife, making a home comfortable for a man. In her ghostwritten autobiography, *My Story*, published in 1914, she said, 'It was made quite clear that men considered themselves superior to women, and that women apparently acqui- esced in that belief.'

When Emmeline began to be involved in

active sexual politics she described herself as a 'conscious and confirmed suffragist'. She had been made aware, from when she was tiny, of the meaning of slavery and emancipation. When she was five she had been asked by her parents to collect pennies in a 'lucky bag' for the newly emancipated slaves in the United States. Both her parents were supporters of equal suffrage and Sophia Jane took the monthly *Woman's Suffrage Journal*, edited by Lydia Becker, one of Manchester's foremost suffragists. When Emmeline was fourteen she asked her mother to take her to a meeting where Becker was speaking – she found the speaker's ideas most engaging.

It was around this time, in late 1872, that Emmeline was sent to study in Paris. Her closest friend was a girl whose father was a famous republican who was imprisoned in New Caledonia for his part in the Paris Commune. Emmeline became a confirmed Francophile and found his story and Thomas Carlyle's popular book *The French Revolution* an inspiration throughout her life. Carlyle's work seems to revel in the violence of the revolutionary terror and welcomes the destruction of the old order in French society. Emmeline would never go so far as to advocate the guillotine for those who opposed her; indeed her suffragettes would be encouraged to damage property without harming human life, but she had learned that change can be achieved by violent revolution.

When she returned to Manchester from France she was almost nineteen and expected by her mother to fall in line in the way a respectable young lady should. Emmeline was not one to waste her energies on boring household tasks and made her view plain to her mother on numerous occasions. There were constant rows between the two women, best illustrated by the afternoon when Mrs Goulden demanded that her daughter should go and fetch her brother's slippers and help make him comfortable. 'No way,' was Emmeline's response. 'If he wants his slippers he can go and get them himself. As for you, mother, if, as you claim, you are truly in favour of women's rights, you are certainly not showing it at home.'

Emmeline began to work with the women's suffrage movement and met a man who was a well-known radical lawyer and supporter of the women's cause. He was Dr Richard Marsden Pankhurst and, despite the twenty-year age gap, they fell in love and married in 1879.

Their four children, Christabel, Sylvia, Henry Francis (known as Frank) and Adela, were born in the first six years of their marriage and while Emmeline's involvement in public affairs was slowed down by motherhood, it far from stopped. In 1880 she was elected onto the committee of the Manchester National Society for Women's Suffrage and was asked to join the Married Women's Property Committee. She and her husband worked together closely on these committees and she campaigned twice on his behalf in 1883 and 1885 when he stood as an independent parliamentary candidate. They proposed the abolition of the House of Lords and the monarchy, adult suffrage on equal terms for both sexes, the disestablishment of the Church of England, nationalisation of land and Home Rule for Ireland. Pretty radical stuff! Pankhurst was not elected.

In 1886 the family left Manchester for London and set up home in Hampstead Road. Emmeline was keen to have financial independence and to support her husband materially so that he could concentrate on his politics, so she opened a shop selling fancy goods. There were frequent trips to Manchester on political business and it was during one of those visits that four-year-old Frank fell ill. When the parents arrived home he was critical. He had been wrongly diagnosed with croup, which turned out to be diphtheria, and he died in September 1888.

The cause of his illness may have been faulty drainage at the rear of the house in Hampstead, so the family closed the shop and moved to a rented house at 8 Russell Square. It was there that her fifth child was born. He was also called Henry Francis in memory of his older brother, but was known as Harry.

8 Russell Square became a centre for radical politics where Fabians – members of the Fabian Society, Britain's oldest political think tank, founded in 1884 to develop public policy on the left – anarchists, socialists and suffragists would meet. The Pankhursts developed a close friendship with the Scottish socialist Keir Hardie, who was elected to Parliament as an Independent MP for West Ham South in 1892. He helped form the Independent Labour Party (ILP) the following year and in 1900 the Labour Party was born. Hardie was the first Labour Member of Parliament when he was elected that year as the junior member for the dual-member constituency of Merthyr Tydfil and Aberdare. He

would represent the constituency for the rest of his life.

In 1893 the Pankhurst family went back to Manchester to 4 Buckingham Crescent. Emmeline resigned from the Women's Liberal Association to join the ILP and in 1894 she was elected as an ILP member to the Chorlton Board of Guardians. The work involved the inspection of workhouses and she was often horrified by the terrible conditions she found there, particularly where girls and single women with babies were concerned. She was described as compassionate and fearless, and managed to introduce a number of improvements.

Her first brush with the law came in 1896 when some of her fellow members of the ILP were sent to prison for giving political speeches in the open air at Boggart Hole Clough, a large urban park, which was owned by Manchester City Council. The Pankhursts and their children were all involved in speaking out in defence of free speech, often appearing in the Clough, and she would shout that she was prepared to go to prison herself. She was taken to court but the case against her was dismissed. Confronted by such opposition to her beliefs, and to her right to speak in public, Emmeline's association with the ILP grew even stronger. In 1897 she was elected to the party's National Administrative Council.

The following year her beloved husband died suddenly as a result of stomach ulcers. He was only sixty-two. His legal practice had never made much money because his close association with the socialist movement had made him an unpopular choice for a great many potential clients. Emmeline and the children were left to struggle financially, and she refused any charitable help from political friends and associates. Instead she asked that donations should be made to build a hall in her husband's memory in Salford.

Meanwhile, she moved the family to cheaper accommodation in 62 Nelson Street, which is now the home of the Pankhurst Centre, a small museum celebrating the birth of the suffragette movement. There was another failed attempt at opening a shop to earn money to keep the family from poverty and finally Emmeline accepted a salaried post as registrar of births and deaths in Chorlton. This work brought her into contact with working-class women who had come to register the births of their babies. They were often young, unmarried girls who had been abused by relatives or employers, and her determination that women must improve their position in society grew ever stronger.

It was five years after Richard's death that the Pankhurst Hall in Salford was finally opened as the headquarters for the local branch of the ILP. Only one problem. It had been decided that women would not be allowed to join the party there. Emmeline immediately left the ILP in protest at what she saw as a waste of her commitment and time to the socialist movement. She became convinced that the only solution for women was to found their own political party.

In her autobiography she wrote, 'It was in October, 1903, that I invited a number of women to my house in Nelson Street, Manchester, for the purposes of organisation. We voted to call our new society the Women's Social and Political Union.' It was agreed the organisation would be open to women of any class and its focus would be a campaign to win votes for women, with the motto 'Deeds not Words'. A few years later, in 1908, the WSPU adopted a colour scheme of purple, white and green, symbolising dignity, purity and hope.

The suffragettes were, from the beginning, adept at publicity and self-promotion,
understanding the need for a slogan and an
identifiable colour scheme. Money would
be raised from the sale of scarves and hats in
suffragette colours, and from postcards and
booklets whose sense of humour often matched
those of the *Punch* cartoons, but told the other
side of the woman question. The suffragettes
clearly showed the positive side of the emancipation of women, whereas the *Punch* cartoonists
invariably portrayed it as a potential disaster
for hearth and home.

The first notable campaign carried out by
the WSPU, after a number of peaceful appear-
ances at trade unions' conferences and street
demonstrations, came in the autumn of 1905
on the eve of a general election, when it was
expected the Liberals would win. Emmeline's
oldest daughter, Christabel, and Annie Kenney,
a working-class Manchester woman, went to a
Liberal Party meeting at the Free Trade Hall
(now a posh hotel) and asked a question: 'Will
the Liberal government, if returned, give votes
to women?' No one answered their question,
so they asked it again. They were bundled
out of the hall, charged with obstruction and

sentenced to pay a fine or go to prison. Emmeline offered to pay their fines, but the two refused and were imprisoned for several days. It proved the turning point in the suffrage campaign. As a result of extensive newspaper coverage, Deeds not Words got noticed.

In 1907 the WSPU moved its headquarters to London and Emmeline left her job as registrar of births and deaths, her only source of income. She now had no settled home and lived in various rented flats, hotels or homes of friends, but was awarded a stipend of £200 per annum from WSPU funds.

Emmeline Pethick-Lawrence became treasurer of the organisation in 1906. She and her husband, Frederick, were wealthy businesspeople and she brought those skills and some personal money to the Union. Donations from supporters were often generous, and at some meetings, where the charismatic Mrs Pankhurst spoke, as much as £14,000 could be raised. Money, jewels and other valuables were frequently thrown onto the platform.

Emmeline Pankhurst's first experience of prison came early in 1908 when she led a deputation to the House of Commons and they were arrested for obstruction. She served a month in what was known as the second division, reserved for common criminal offenders, rather than the first division for political prisoners. Later that same year, in October, she was back in the dock in Bow Street, accused of incitement to disorder with Christabel and Flora Drummond – a WSPU organiser known as 'The General' because of the uniform she chose to wear. They had published a handbill encouraging a 'rush' on the House of Commons. The three women defended themselves in court. Emmeline's speech in her defence and her description in the dock of the miserable lives led by so many women moved people to tears. Nevertheless, she was sentenced to three months in jail.

Prison became a familiar home for suffragettes who had taken part in angry and impatient demonstrations. In 1909 members decided that they would go on hunger strike in an attempt to persuade the authorities that they should be treated not as common criminals but as *political* prisoners. Their demands were not met. Instead, force-feeding began where a tube would be pushed down a weak and hungry prisoner's throat and sustenance poured into the stomach, an extremely painful practice. Emmeline was horrified and condemned the government for torturing women who had merely expressed a justifiable grievance. The force-feeding continued, but, of course, publicity and sympathy came as a result.

Emmeline left for the United States in October that same year and was greeted enthusiastically wherever she spoke, particularly at Carnegie Hall in New York. She opened her speech with, 'I am what you call a hooligan.' She was a brilliant orator, always able to demonstrate the most important qualities for an effective speaker – 'Make 'em laugh, make 'em cry, make 'em think.'

Her triumphant conquering of America and Canada raised much-needed funds for the WSPU coffers, but she was to face tragedy on her return. Her surviving son, Harry, had developed an inflammation of the spinal cord, which had left him paralysed from the waist down. In January 1910 he died; Sylvia said that her mother was broken emotionally by his death. Emmeline then threw herself into the general election campaign of that year and followed the Union's policy of opposing each and every Liberal candidate, regardless of his attitude for or against the enfranchisement of women.

The Liberal government did win the election, but with a greatly reduced majority. The Liberals had 275 seats, the Conservatives 273, the Irish Nationalists 82 and Labour 40. A left-wing journalist, Henry Brailsford, who was sympathetic to the women's cause (he had resigned from his job at the *Daily News* because the paper had supported the force-feeding of suffragette hunger strikers) thought the make-up of a hung Parliament, with the balance of power held by Labour and the Irish, might offer a better opportunity for successful lobbying. He formed a Conciliation Committee for Women's Suffrage and for the time being Emmeline called a halt to militant action.

The committee came up with the Women's Franchise Bill. In order that the Conservatives should not be frightened off, its demands were narrow. It sought to extend the vote to independent female property owners, but would exclude women whose husbands met the property qualification. Very few women would have won the vote in those circumstances and Emmeline was opposed to the Bill in principle, but was furious when, after passing a

Second Reading, it was opposed by the Home Secretary, David Lloyd George, and by the Prime Minister, Herbert Asquith.

When Parliament reassembled no reference was made to the Bill. The WSPU organised a deputation of protest to the House of Commons on 18 November. The police brutality on that day led to it being called Black Friday. Around 300 women joined the protest and 119 were arrested. Many protesters were attacked by the police and two women later died of their injuries. There were allegations of sexual assault against a number of officers, but none of them were pursued. Four days later Emmeline organised another march, this time to Downing Street. Among the 156 women arrested on that occasion were Emmeline and her sister, Mary. No evidence was offered against Emmeline so she avoided prison on this occasion, but Mary died at Christmas as a result of the injuries she had suffered at the hands of the police on Black Friday.

There was much toing and froing around a revised Conciliation Bill when the second 1910 election was announced for December of that year. The WSPU felt it could support

the Bill now as it included all women householders. Militant action was again suspended
and Emmeline made another speaking trip
to North America. During her absence she
discovered the Prime Minister had announced
that a Manhood Suffrage Bill would be introduced in the next session that would broaden
men's enfranchisement. He said it would
allow an amendment for women. Such an
amendment could not be carried without the
support of the government, which Emmeline
was convinced would not be forthcoming.
She returned to London on 18 January 1912,
according to Sylvia, speaking of 'Sedition!' and
'The Women's Revolution'.

In February 1912, at a meeting to welcome
back newly released prisoners, Emmeline
announced a new policy. She had decided
that reasoned argument, speeches, marches,
demonstrations and chaining oneself to the
railings of the House of Commons were getting
them nowhere. Instead, the stone would serve
as the weapon and replace the argument
at the next demonstration. She had lessons
in stone-throwing from the composer Ethel
Smyth (see vignette at the end of this book) and
the WSPU struck for the first time, without

warning, on 1 March, smashing windows in the West End of London.

Later that afternoon she and two other women broke windows in Downing Street and two more days of window-smashing followed. In court she argued that women had failed to get the vote because they had failed to employ the methods of disruption often used by men. She was sentenced to several months in prison, but released after a few days in order to attend a new trial with the Pethick-Lawrences, charged with conspiracy. Christabel had escaped to Paris.

Again Emmeline made political speeches from the dock, arguing that women had been driven to violence by the opposition of the government. The three defendants were found guilty and sentenced to nine months in the second division, with common criminals. They threatened hunger strike if they were not sent, as political prisoners, to the first division. Their demand was granted, but it was not extended to other suffrage prisoners. The three leaders joined the others in a mass hunger strike and again force-feeding began. Emmeline resisted the doctor and the warders when they came to her cell. When she picked up a heavy earthenware jug and threatened to defend herself if they came near her, they withdrew. She was released on medical grounds two days later and was never threatened with force-feeding again.

Emmeline spent some time travelling to see Christabel in France using the name Mrs Richards. She cut back on her speaking engagements and spent more time in London at WSPU's headquarters. There was a major rift between her and the Pethick-Lawrences: Emmeline was keen to increase the programme of militant action; the Pethick-Lawrences were not. Emmeline and Christabel told them, perhaps rather brutally given the unwavering support they had provided for so long, that their services were no longer required.

It was an unwise move in the long term. A number of WSPU members were furious that the couple had been so dismissed. Some of Emmeline's followers retained their faith in her leadership, but the WSPU lost a lot of its rich and influential supporters, and it now fell to her to take over the job of treasurer and fundraiser, the work that had been carried out so effectively by Mrs Pethick-Lawrence.

Mrs Pankhurst, with the revolutionary bit between her teeth, announced a new plan for militant action at a meeting at the Royal Albert Hall on 17 October 1912. She emphasised that the WSPU would support no political party and that the 'revolution' would now include attacks on both public and private property. There must, she said, be no danger to human life, but that it was just to attack the things she considered were most valued by society – 'money, property and pleasure'. 'Militancy is right,' she concluded, 'because no measure worth having has been won in any other way.'

The militant action escalated with such tactics as setting fire to pillar boxes, raising false fire alarms, attacking works of art – Mary Richardson famously slashed Velázquez's *Rokeby Venus* in the National Gallery – severing telegraph and telephone wires, and damaging golf courses. No human life was put at risk during these activities, but there is one attack, which took place in 1913, where the suffragettes were extremely lucky that no one was killed or injured.

On 20 February *The Times* reported, 'An attempt was made yesterday morning to blow up the house which is being built for Mr. Lloyd George near Walton Heath Golf Links.' One device had exploded, causing some £500 worth of damage. Another had failed to go off. That evening, at a meeting in Cardiff, Mrs Pankhurst made a confession. 'We have blown up the Chancellor of the Exchequer's house . . . [F]or all that has been done in the past, I accept responsibility. That I have advised, I have incited, I have conspired.'

Lloyd George saw the action as an act of terrorism, as he told Sir George Riddell, the proprietor of the *News of the World*. Sir George wrote of the conversation in his diary:

> L. G. much interested. Said the facts had not been brought out and that no proper point had been made of the fact that the bombs had been concealed in cupboards, which must have resulted in the death of twelve men had not the bomb which first exploded blown out the candle attached to the second bomb which had not been discovered, hidden away as it was.

The workmen had been due to arrive at 6 a.m. to carry on working on the house.

Christabel, interviewed in Paris where she was hiding from the possibility of prosecution, was asked if the WSPU minded being described as anarchists. 'We do not mind at all,' she replied, 'we are fighting a revolution.' She explained that Lloyd George was a primary target because, while often claiming to be in favour of women's suffrage, 'he was always betraying us'.

The perpetrators of the bombing were never caught, but, because of Emmeline's public confession, she was arrested for procuring and inciting women to commit offences contrary to the Malicious Injuries to Property Act. On 3 April 1913 she was sentenced to three years' penal servitude and immediately went on hunger strike.

There was no attempt to feed her forcibly and a new law was rapidly introduced to ensure she did not die in prison and become a martyr for the cause. The Prisoners (Temporary Discharge for Ill-Health) Bill was rushed through to enable prisoners on hunger strike to be released when their health began to fail, give them time to recover and then return them to prison. It came to be known as the Cat and Mouse Act.

In August 1914, as the First World War began, the WSPU suspended its campaign. A letter to members said, 'Even the most vigorous militancy is rendered less effective by contrast with the infinitely greater violence done in the present war.' *The Suffragette*, the newspaper that had been edited by Christabel, was renamed *Britannia* with 'For King, For Country, For Freedom' as its slogan.

Emmeline campaigned for the widening of work available to women in support of the war effort and she, together with a number of other WSPU members, accepted the request of Lloyd George to organise a Women's Right to Serve demonstration to help overcome trade union opposition to the employment of female labourers. Lloyd George was the first senior politician to occupy the newly created post of Minister of Munitions, a job he held from 1915 to 1916. He was so successful at increasing the production of shells for the battlefield – work which included female labourers – that he boosted morale and raised his profile, contributing to his rise to Prime Minister in December 1916.

His elevation to the top job encouraged the suffragists to restore the campaign for women to have the right to vote in 1917. Asquith, the previous Prime Minister, had been implacably opposed to women's enfranchisement. Lloyd George, they thought, had dillied and dallied and made promises which had not been fulfilled, but they believed him, essentially, to have sympathy for the cause. The suffragists lobbied the coalition government like mad to ensure that women – or at least those over the age of thirty – would be included in the proposed new Representation of the People Bill.

The WSPU was renamed in 1917 as the Women's Party. *Britannia* became its official newspaper, edited by Christabel. On 6 February 1918 Royal Assent was given to the Act, which allowed women over the age of thirty the vote if they were householders, the wives of householders, occupiers of property with an annual rent of £5 or more, or graduates of British universities. Only 8.5 million women were included, but it was clear to all the suffrage campaigners that the first step had been taken and full citizenship for all women could not be far away.

Emmeline was keen that Christabel should become the first female Member of Parliament. Of her three daughters it was only Christabel who was in tune with their mother's politics. She fought the Smethwick constituency on the Women's Party ticket in the autumn general election and lost, but narrowly.

In 1924, after a hectic time during which Emmeline had lectured on social hygiene in Canada, where there were terrible worries about the number of men returning from the war with venereal infections, her health began to fail. She was sixty-six and had added to her responsibilities by taking in a small group of girls who had been orphaned during the war. It proved too much for her. Two of the girls were given up for adoption by well-off families, Christabel adopted one of the others, Betty, while another, Mary, stayed with Emmeline until 1928.

Emmeline returned to London in 1925 and was invited to stand as a Conservative candidate. She accepted the offer of the socialist working-class district of Whitechapel and St George's, knowing she couldn't win. When she was campaigning in the spring of 1928 she was shocked to learn from the *News of the World* that Sylvia had given birth to a son out of wedlock. She was heckled during her campaign about her immoral and wayward daughter, but dismissed the comments by saying she would not discuss private matters in public. She was never reconciled with Sylvia and saw her behaviour as an absolute disgrace. Adela had already gone to live in Australia. Only Christabel remained close to her mother.

In late May of 1928 Emmeline became very ill and was taken to a nursing home at 43 Wimpole Street where she died on 14 June from septicaemia contracted after a bout of flu. She was a month short of her seventieth birthday and only a couple of weeks away from seeing the full enfranchisement she had worked so hard to achieve. On 2 July 1928 the second Representation of the People Act gave voting rights to women over the age of twenty-one on equal terms with men.

Emmeline Pankhurst was buried in Brompton Cemetery in London and in March 1930 the Conservative Prime Minister, Stanley Baldwin, unveiled a bronze statue of her in Victoria Tower Gardens. It's a public park close to the River Thames and adjacent to the Victoria Tower on the south-western corner of the Palace of Westminster.

There she is, to be remembered forever, close to the Houses of Parliament, whose closed doors she had made such efforts to open to women and win for us all the right to take our place as full citizens of Britain.

'I do wish your lot had the decency
to shoot me.'

Constance Markievicz

5

Constance
Markievicz

1868–1927

I t's often assumed that Nancy Astor was the first woman elected to the British Parliament in 1919. She was indeed the first female MP to occupy her seat in the House of Commons, as we'll see in the next chapter, but the first to be elected was Constance Markievicz, who won her seat in the 1918 general election, but, as a member of Sinn Féin, she obeyed the Irish Republican Party's policy of abstention and never attended.

Constance Georgina Gore-Booth was one of four children born to Sir Henry Gore-Booth of Lissadell in County Sligo and his wife, Georgina Mary. The Gore-Booths were a wealthy English family who had owned land in Sligo since the seventeenth century. They were not, though, the kind of absentee landlords who had so abandoned their Irish peasant workers during the Famine of the mid-nineteenth century. Constance was raised by parents who taught her to care for and respect those less fortunate than themselves.

And the Gore-Booth girls were indeed fortunate. They were cultured, sporty and beautiful, and she and her sister, Eva, had a very close relationship. They inspired W. B. Yeats who, in 1927, wrote 'In Memory of Eva Gore-Booth and Con Markiewicz', describing the sisters as 'Two girls in silk kimonos, both / Beautiful, one a gazelle.'

Like their contemporaries in the late nineteenth century, the girls were educated at home and taught music, poetry and art. In 1887 they were taken by their governess on a typically aristocratic grand tour of Europe and, upon their return, were expected to fulfil their duties as good, high-class girls. They would be presented at court, make good marriages and spend the rest of their lives as wives, mothers and society hostesses. Constance was presented to Queen Victoria at Buckingham Palace in 1887, but neither she nor her sister did what was expected of a debutante. Constance had plenty of offers of a 'suitable' marriage, but turned down all her suitors. Like so many women, she had to fight her family to achieve what she wanted. She was determined, she told her father, to study art and in 1893 he relented and she was enrolled in the Slade School of Fine Art in London.

The women's suffrage movement was beginning to bubble – only ten years later the Women's Social and Political Union would be founded – and Constance was drawn to the arguments of the suffragists. By 1896 she was presiding over a meeting of the Sligo Women's Suffrage Society.

In 1898 she went to Paris to carry on studying art and it was there she met Count Casimir Dunin-Markievicz, a wealthy Polish national whose family owned land in Ukraine. They married in 1900, had their only child, a daughter, Maeve, in 1901 and then returned to Dublin as a family in 1902. The two of them became involved in Dublin's cultural and political life. Casimir and Constance produced and acted in plays at the Abbey Theatre, helped found the United Arts Club and exhibited their own artistic work.

Constance's political life became increasingly radical after she rented a cottage in the countryside outside Dublin in 1906. A set of leaflets had been left behind by a previous tenant. The title of the series of pamphlets was 'The Peasant and Sinn Féin' and the text advocated independence from British rule. She was soon persuaded of the cause.

Constance was introduced in 1908 to Helena Molony and an organisation called Inghinidhe na hÉireann (Daughters of Ireland). Molony had been spurred into feminist and republican activity by Maud Gonne, the English-born revolutionary, suffragette, actor and inspiring speaker, perhaps best remembered for her turbulent relationship with Yeats.

The group had grown from a campaign to organise a 'patriotic children's treat' for children who boycotted Queen Victoria's visit to Ireland in 1900. It warned girls against consorting with British soldiers, pressed local shops into stocking Irish rather than British goods and set out to persuade boys that the British Army was not a suitable career. Constance was a founder of the monthly newspaper published by the group, *Bean na hÉireann* (*Women of Ireland*), said to be committed to 'militancy, separatism and feminism'. She wrote articles about gardening for the publication. She also joined Sinn Féin.

In 1909 Constance played an important role in the formation of the Irish Boy Scouts Movement. Its stated aim was to train boys in drill and the firing of rifles, teach them to engage with the Irish language and culture, and prepare themselves to help in the establishment of an independent and united Ireland. By 1911 she was a member of the executive of Sinn Féin and was arrested while protesting against the visit of King George V to Dublin.

Constance's politics began to move further to the left and she worked closely with James Connolly in the growing trade union movement. In 1911 she spoke at the meeting to establish the Irish Women Workers' Union and her house in Rathmines, a suburb to the south of Dublin, became a hotbed of nationalist and trade union activity. During the 1913 Lockout, where some twenty thousand workers had entered into dispute with around three hundred employers, she organised a soup kitchen in Liberty Hall and joined the newly founded Irish Citizen Army, a voluntary group of trade union members trained to protect the demonstrators.

By 1914 Constance realised revolution was brewing and she was instrumental in the merging of the two main women's organisations, Cumann na mBan and Inghinidhe na hÉireann, into one. Cumann na mBan, the Irishwomen's Council, began to define itself as an Irish women's paramilitary organisation, which in 1916 became an auxiliary of the Irish Volunteers, the group led by Éamon de Valera that would become the Irish Republican Army (IRA).

At the outbreak of the Great War she and her husband separated. He went to the Balkans to work as a war reporter and their daughter went to Sligo to be cared for by her grandparents, leaving Constance free to pursue her political aims. She had no difficulties in espousing military action to break Ireland's link with Britain, and by 1916 she was ready to be an active participant in the Easter Rising.

On Easter Monday, 24 April 1916, Constance loaded up Dr Kathleen Lynn's car with first aid kits and, as she described it, 'drove off through quiet dusty streets and across the river, reaching City Hall'. She reported to Michael Mallin who was second in command of the Irish Citizen Army and in charge of the St Stephen's Green Garrison. The occupation of St Stephen's Green, the public park at the centre of Dublin, was already well under way. She remained there for a week, effectively becoming Mallin's deputy. She organised the defence of the park and is reputed to have shot a policeman. By early Tuesday the situation of the rebels in St Stephen's Green was deteriorating. The British had taken control of the buildings surrounding the park, including the Shelbourne Hotel.

The garrison came under increasing fire, so they retreated to the Royal College of Surgeons where they would spend the rest of the week. On the Sunday morning, Elizabeth O'Farrell, a nurse and prominent member of the Irishwomen's Council, led the surrender. She walked from Grafton Street towards the college, carrying a white flag. She handed the surrender note to Markievicz who read it and handed it in turn to Mallin. O'Farrell took the note to the other volunteer outposts in the city, Mallin ordered the white flag to be flown from the college and Captain Henry de Courcy-Wheeler – a distant relative of the Gore-Booths – arrived to accept the surrender. He met Mallin and Markievicz at the college door. She kissed her pistol and handed it to the Captain before being marched to Richmond Barracks along with her fellow insurgents.

Markievicz was the only woman tried in a court martial after the Easter Rising. She defended herself in court by saying, 'I went out for Ireland's freedom and it doesn't matter what happens to me. I did what I thought was right and I stand by it.' She was sentenced to death, but it was decided that, because of her gender, her sentence would be commuted to life imprisonment. It's said the British government had been criticised so often for the cruel treatment of suffragettes during the force-feeding period that they were afraid to execute a prominent woman.

No such sentiment applied to the male rebel leaders. Her commander during the rising, Michael Mallin, was executed by firing squad on 8 May 1916. He was forty-one and left a family including his mother, three siblings, a pregnant wife and four children. Constance heard the firing squads do their work from her cell and is reported to have said, 'I do wish your lot had the decency to shoot me.'

She was transferred from Kilmainham Gaol to Mountjoy and then to Aylesbury Prison in England. She took instruction in Catholicism while in prison and was released under the general amnesty in June 1917, having served fourteen months of her life sentence.

Markievicz soon resumed her political activities. She was elected again to the executive of Sinn Féin and became president of Cumann na mBan. In 1918 she was arrested again for alleged involvement in the 'German plot'. The Dublin Castle administration in Ireland claimed a conspiracy had been hatched between the Sinn Féin movement and the German Empire to start an armed insurrection in Ireland during the Great War.

There was no hard evidence that such a plot existed; indeed it's now generally regarded as a 'black propaganda' project to discredit Sinn Féin. The arrests proved counter-productive for the British. The more accommodating members of the Sinn Féin leadership were caught and imprisoned, while those more committed to physical force had been forewarned and escaped. The whole incident enabled

Michael Collins to consolidate his control of Sinn Féin and put the IRA on a more focused military footing to continue the guerrilla war of Irish independence, which went on from January 1919 to July 1921.

It was during her second period of residing at His Majesty's Pleasure that Constance stood for election as a Sinn Féin candidate for Dublin's St Patrick's division in the 1918 general election. She won, becoming the first woman elected to the British Parliament, but never took her seat. She was released from prison in March 1919 and was appointed Minister of Labour in the first Irish Parliament – the Dáil Éireann, which declared itself independent from Britain. There would not be another woman minister in the Irish Parliament until Máire Geoghegan-Quinn was appointed to the Cabinet by Charles Haughey in 1979.

Her fighting spirit had not been quelled by the experiences following 1916. She continued her opposition to British rule in Ireland and was arrested in 1919 for making a seditious speech and sentenced to four months' hard labour. In September 1920 she was arrested again and, this time, sentenced to two years' hard labour. She was released in July 1921 during the truce when de Valera and Lloyd George negotiated the Anglo-Irish Treaty.

Constance was vehemently opposed to the Treaty and gave a storming performance in the Dáil, condemning it and advocating an Irish Workers' Republic. She took the side of the Anti-Treaty IRA during the Civil War, which lasted from June 1922 to May 1923. It ended with victory for those in favour of the Treaty and the foundation of the Irish Free State.

Constance was re-elected to the Dáil in 1923, but refused to take the Oath of Allegiance to the British crown, so, again, didn't take her seat in Parliament. Later that year she was arrested for the fourth time because she'd been trying to collect signatures for a petition demanding the release of republican prisoners. In jail she went on hunger strike until she and her fellow prisoners were released.

In 1926 de Valera formed Fianna Fáil, a centre-right republican party which split from Sinn Féin on the issue of abstentionism – the very reason Constance, as a Sinn Féin member, had refused her seats in the British Parliament and the Dáil. She broke her ties with Sinn Féin and Cumann na mBan and joined Fianna Fáil. It's unclear why her militancy was tempered, but in 1927, during the general election, she campaigned and was elected to the Dáil as a Fianna Fáil candidate.

Her long years of fighting, terms in prison and hunger strikes had begun to take their toll on her health. The previous year, during a coal strike, she had spent her time trudging around Dublin bringing food and fuel to the city's poor. Her sister Eva had died that year and Constance was beset by grief, and she quickly became extremely ill after the death of her closest companion. In 1927 she was admitted to Sir Patrick Dun's hospital, insisting on being cared for in the public ward as a pauper. She was fifty-nine when she died in July.

She lay in state in the Pillar Room of the Rotunda Rink in Dublin where the Irish Volunteers had been launched. It was a temporary building in the Rotunda Gardens that could hold four thousand people, and many thousands went there to pay their respects to 'their countess'. Her funeral oration was delivered by Éamon de Valera and she was buried at Glasnevin Cemetery, Dublin.

The great playwright Séan O'Casey, who lived through and documented the war of independence in plays such as *The Shadow of a Gunman*, *The Plough and the Stars* and *Juno and the Paycock*, wrote of Constance Markievicz, 'One thing she had in abundance was physical courage: with that she was clothed as with a garment.' Her bravery and passion for the politics of an independent Ireland cannot be denied.

'He told me they hoped to freeze
me out. It felt, he said, like a
woman had entered his bathroom
and he had nothing to protect
himself apart from his sponge. I
told him he was not handsome
enough to have such fears!'

Nancy Astor on Churchill

6

Nancy Astor

1879–1964

I first encountered the wit and wisdom of Nancy Astor and the controversies and inconsistencies that often surrounded her during her political life when, in 2000, *Woman's Hour* broadcast an interview from the archive that she had given in 1956. The reason for the repeat was the eightieth anniversary of her maiden speech in the House of Commons. She was the first woman to take her seat in the British Parliament when she won the by-election in Plymouth Sutton in 1919.

Her husband, the millionaire Waldorf Astor, was American-born, but naturalised British. He had held the Plymouth seat, but when his father Viscount Astor died, Waldorf inherited his peerage, was forced to resign his seat and joined the House of Lords. Nancy agreed to stand in his place.

Nancy was also American, born as Nancy Witcher Langhorne. She was the eighth of eleven children of a Virginian railway business-man, Chiswell Langhorne, and his wife, Nancy. The family had not been wealthy when Nancy was born as her father's business, which is thought to have depended on slave labour, had folded as a result of the American Civil War. He worked hard to rebuild their resources, and by the time Nancy was thirteen they were a rich family again with a substantial estate in Albemarle County, Virginia.

Nancy and her sister Irene were sent to a finishing school in New York. It's curious that her expensive and high-quality education did nothing to temper her Virginian accent. In the 1956 interview, after years of living in England and mixing with the social crème de la crème, 'going to' still becomes 'gonna', 'them' is ''em' and she seems incapable of placing an 'ing' at the end of a word that requires it. Thus 'flirting' is 'flirtin'' and 'going' is 'goin''.

In New York she met her first husband, a

wealthy socialite called Robert Gould Shaw, and they were married when Nancy was only eighteen. It was a disastrously unhappy marriage. They had one son, Robert Gould Shaw III, but her husband, according to their friends, was an alcoholic and an abuser. He was accused of raping and beating his wife.

They stayed together for four years. Nancy left him numerous times, the first time on their honeymoon, but kept going back. She left for good in 1901 and they were finally divorced in 1903. Her divorce coincided with the death of her mother and she went home to Virginia with the intention of running the estate. She did not prove a success at this and her father encouraged her to travel. She fell in love with England and decided to move to London permanently with her sister Phyllis in 1905.

It was not uncommon at the time for impoverished English aristocrats to marry wealthy Americans for their money. Unsurprisingly, Nancy was asked by an English woman at a social event, 'Have you come to get our husbands?' Nancy's response was, 'If you knew the trouble I had getting rid of mine . . . you'd know I don't want yours.' It's the first recorded example of the cutting wit for which she became famous and it seems to have gone down extremely well with the perhaps more reserved London socialites. She was beautiful, charming and funny – she was a hit.

Her marriage to Waldorf Astor took place in 1906 and lasted until his death in 1952. He had moved to England with his family at the age of twelve and had been raised as an English aristocrat. They were extremely well matched, even sharing the same birthday, 19 May 1879. The house they moved into after the wedding is now considered one of the most beautiful in England. Cliveden is an Italianate mansion and estate, which was a wedding gift from Waldorf's father. They also had a grand London house at 4 St James's Square in Westminster. Cliveden is huge and sits on the banks of the River Thames in Buckinghamshire. Its grounds are stunning and it was only in the twilight of Nancy's life, in 1963, that it became notorious.

It was where a number of incidents in the Profumo affair occurred. Christine Keeler and Mandy Rice Davies were invited to Cliveden as company for the powerful and wealthy men who met there. Keeler had an affair with John Profumo who was then Secretary of State for War. She was also allegedly involved in a dalliance with Yevgeny Ivanov, the Soviet naval attaché, and when the details came out in the press there were serious questions about whether national security had been breached as a result of pillow talk from Profumo to Keeler and thus on to Ivanov. The scandal brought down the Macmillan government and made Cliveden famous for all the wrong reasons. It has now restored its reputation, in a way. It's owned by the National Trust and is leased as a five-star hotel.

Nancy's son William, the third Viscount Astor, was accused of having an affair with Mandy Rice Davies. When she was told in court that he had denied the accusation Mandy gave her famous response, 'Well, he would, wouldn't he?' In Peter Stanford's book about the affair, Bronwen Astor, William's wife, lays the blame for her husband's 'little boy lost' persona on his domineering, possessive and formidable mother, who spoiled and indulged him at every turn. I guess it's always the mother who gets the blame.

In her interview with *Woman's Hour* Nancy was asked about her wealth and whether there was a degree of shame or criticism attached to being fabulously rich as a politician who concerned herself with the poor, particularly poverty-stricken children. Her answer was unequivocal:

I adore bein' rich. During an election campaign someone yelled out one night, 'Mr Astor's a millionaire, ain't he!' Mr Astor was embarrassed, but I replied, 'I hope to God he is. It's one of the reasons I married him. Now come out an' show your face.' It seems to me most extraordinary that anyone should be ashamed of it.

One rich woman went to the East End and put on her worst clothes. When I went to the East End I would have considered it rude not to wear my good clothes. People know you've got 'em. I think what people hate is pretence. Nobody is more proud of the progress in this country than I am and my contribution to it. What a joy it is not to see ragged children and children with their feet out.

Her constituents in Plymouth were, on the whole, remarkably tolerant about her wealth, knowing perhaps that her husband's family were well-respected philanthropists in the area. In her papers there are numerous letters from women detailing their hardships in the 1930s and evidence that Nancy sent them money. Not all her riches were given to good causes, though. There are in the same papers from the same period phenomenal bills from her jewellers and couturiers in London and Paris, and details of huge amounts of money spent on lavish entertaining in both London and at Cliveden.

By the time Nancy decided she would stand for Parliament in the by-election after her husband transferred from the Commons to the Lords, she and Waldorf had five children plus the son from her first marriage. She was asked, inevitably, during the campaign whether she should not be at home looking after her children. 'I feel someone ought to be looking after the unfortunate children,' she replied. 'My children are among the fortunate ones.'

Nancy campaigned enthusiastically and silenced her hecklers with rapid repartee. One who shouted out during one of her speeches, 'Call yourself a lady?' received the response, 'Certainly not!' She became the Conservative

MP for Plymouth Sutton with a majority of 5,203 votes. In her election address she talked about how she had 'no personal ambition to go to Parliament' but had been encouraged by others. 'I intend,' she said, 'to work for the Peace, Progress and Prosperity of the country. I shall, at the same time, have due regard to National Efficiency and Economy which women above all understand.'

She took her seat in the House on 1 December 1919, led in between Arthur Balfour and Lloyd George. She received hundreds of letters of congratulation, but none from the suffragist movement. Constance Markievicz described her as 'of the upper classes and out of touch'. Christabel Pankhurst and a number of other women from the movement had stood in 1918 and none had been successful. There was a lot of anger that the first woman to make it was an extremely wealthy American with no political background at all. She was asked on *Woman's Hour* how it had felt to be that first woman, going there all alone.

Of course the suffragettes were disappointed. They didn't know me and had hoped for one of their own. Nobody was more distressed

than I to be the first woman in the House.
I'm a proud Virginian and would not have
wanted an Englishwoman to be the first in
my legislature. I apologised to Mrs Fawcett
and so on. But the loyalty of the women
surpassed all expectations.

How did I feel that first day? Well, I didn't
mind the election at all. I liked that, but
to walk up to the House between Arthur
Balfour and Lloyd George, both of whom
said they believed in women, but would
rather have had a rattlesnake than me at
that time. It was alarmin'. Sometimes I
would sit for five hours in my seat not darin'
to get down.

What kept me goin'? I was an ardent
feminist. I always knew women have more
moral strength. I said once in the House to
the men we've got moral strength, you've
got immoral strength. It was a bit rude, but
I was often quite rude.

The suffragists and suffragettes soon came to
accept Nancy Astor and recognise her value
to the cause. There were frequent parties in St

James's Square to which they were invited and Nancy was only too well aware of the usefulness of her phenomenal connections.

It's a jolly good thing I was the first. I knew everyone and could make introductions and advance things. I cared about social reform and knew the editors of the press as personal friends to get the ideas out. I could afford good secretaries. So much support to keep me up.

She was extremely isolated, never going to the bars and smoking rooms and wearing a simple uniform of jacket, skirt and white shirt. She explained her way of dressing was studied to give her credibility, and compared herself with some of the women who came in later.

One had a new dress every day, dressed more for Ascot than the House of Commons. And she flirted. Men don't like flirtin' in public. If I had been a sexy woman I wouldn't have lasted a week. Another woman was bustiviferous and the men said that at last they had a mother. I told 'em I had six children and she hadn't. You know they judge mothers by their figures sometimes and it's a mistake. They shouldn't.

Her maiden speech in February 1920 was on what she called 'that vexed question, Drink'. When she had first gone to Plymouth she could count ten public houses in one street. She also had a history of living with a violent drunk and it was not uncommon for temperance to be high on the female agenda, as it was well known that alcohol was at the root of a great deal of domestic violence. She told *Woman's Hour* that she was not a prohibitionist, but believed in encouraging temperance. 'No one thought I'd be re-elected when that was the subject of my maiden speech, but the people of Plymouth were brave. I stuck to Plymouth. Plymouth stuck to me.'

Nancy's majority was reduced in 1922 when the brewers ran an independent candidate against her, but she was returned on a further six occasions, only retiring, reluctantly, and at her husband's request, in 1945. Her most significant legislative achievement was the passing of a law in 1923 prohibiting the sale of alcohol to anyone under the age of eighteen. It was the first piece of legislation resulting from a Private Member's Bill brought by a woman MP.

She also campaigned on a variety of women's issues, including widows' pensions, employment rights, maternal mortality rates, nursery school provision and the raising of the age of consent. She was the only female MP until 1921 and she received up to two thousand letters each week from women asking for her help in raising their concerns.

Curiously, she opposed an equal divorce law, even though she was divorced. Her stance on the subject was one of a number of inconsistencies and was, perhaps, associated with her conversion to Christian Science, a belief system that suited her values of self-reliance and hard work. She did become something of a missionary for her faith and is reputed to have attempted to convert Stalin in 1931. Stalin was having none of it. She was not an entirely faithful adherent to the rules of her church as she is known to have sought medical advice when necessary. The press pilloried her for her opposition to equal divorce.

Nancy always stuck to her guns and was never afraid of the party whips:

This was because women had put me in to represent them. I was concerned with women and children. I felt it was my duty to do it. I wanted the world to get better and it couldn't if it was gonna be ruled by men. I'm amazed how well they did it for two thousand years alone. We know what they are if we leave 'em in the house alone! Why did I have the courage to fight for what I believed in? Because I would tell 'em, I've got the women and you will hear from 'em. And so they did, didn't they? It's amazin' how well the men treated me, considerin' how few wanted me.

As the Second World War approached Nancy and her 'Cliveden Set' became known for their views on appeasement. It was not unusual for members of the aristocracy to oppose war with Germany. Indeed, there are questions over some members of the Royal Family having sympathy with Hitler, as did prominent members of the Mitford family and their high-powered associates. The American Ambassador, Joe Kennedy, was in the appeasement camp and would have been part of the Astors' social circle. Nancy made it clear that, having lived through the Great War, she was simply terrified of another such conflict.

She openly opposed communism and Catholicism, but there is no evidence that she was pro-Nazi, although, like a number of those in the appeasement movement, she had meetings with German officers. She spoke out against their treatment of women and the Nazi ideal of *Kinder, Küche, Kirche* – that women were only suited to attending church, having babies and cooking. At the start of the war she made an apology for having favoured appeasement and voted against Neville Chamberlain, but her reputation was damaged.

I guess in many ways Nancy Astor is best known for her verbal fencing with Winston Churchill, and she didn't always come away with a victory. She told Mr Churchill one evening in the House that he was drunk. He replied, 'And you, madam, are ugly, but tomorrow I shall be sober.' On another occasion she told him that if he were her husband she would poison his tea. To which Churchill replied, 'Madam, if you were my wife, I would drink it.'

When asked about her relationship with Churchill on *Woman's Hour* she talked about a social event where they had met and she had asked him why in her early days in the House he and his fellow MPs had never spoken to her. 'He told me they hoped to freeze me out. It felt, he said, like a woman had entered his bathroom and he had nothing to protect himself apart from his sponge. I told him he was not handsome enough to have such fears!'

Nancy's lasting legacy as an MP is that she quietly and conservatively wormed her way into the House of Commons, working within the sphere of women and children, and didn't frighten the horses. She was an effective model for those who came after her. She was quiet, rarely caused a ruckus, was of the same class as most of the male MPs and gave them a chance to get used to her and to the idea of women being a part of the parliamentary system. Her more forthright sisters followed on.

Nancy died in 1964, and her ashes were interred at the Octagon Temple at Cliveden. Some of her last words sum up the dry wit of the woman who blazed a trail for us all. During her final illness, at her daughter's home in Grimsthorpe Castle in Lincolnshire, her children gathered around her bed. 'Jakie,' she asked, 'is it my birthday, or am I dying?'

Ethel Smyth, composer

1858–1944

Ethel had been a mean bowler in the games of cricket she'd played with her brothers and their friends. It came in handy when Emmeline Pankhurst announced that smashing windows with stones would become a policy of the suffragettes and she needed someone to teach her and her fellow revolutionaries how to throw with accuracy. Ethel was a willing teacher and practitioner, and served a short time in prison for her crime.

During Ethel's enforced stay in Holloway Prison, serving her time for the stone-throwing activities, Thomas Beecham went to visit her and found, on entering the main courtyard, a crowd of suffragettes 'marching around it and singing lustily their war chant while the composer, beaming approbation from an overlooking window, beat time in almost Bacchic frenzy with a toothbrush'.

FORTHCOMING

A History of the World in 21 Women
A Personal Selection

by Jenni Murray

Publishing 6 September 2018

They led while others followed. They stood up and spoke out when no one else would. They broke the mould in art, journalism, politics … Each of them fought, in her own way, for change. *A History of the World in 21 Women* celebrates the lives, struggles and achievements of women who have had a profound impact on the shaping of our world.

Jenni's 21 will be: Joan of Arc, Artemisia Gentileschi, Angela Merkel, Benazir Bhutto, Hillary Clinton, Coco Chanel, Empress Dowager Cixi, Catherine the Great, Clara Schumann, Hatshepsut, Wangari Maathai, Golda Meir, Frida Kahlo, Toni Morrison, Margaret Atwood, Isabella of Castile, Cathy Freeman, Anna Politkovskaya, Sirimavo Bandaranaike, Madonna and Marie Curie.